the complete
contented
cat

Your Ultimate Guide
to Feline Fulfilment

David Taylor

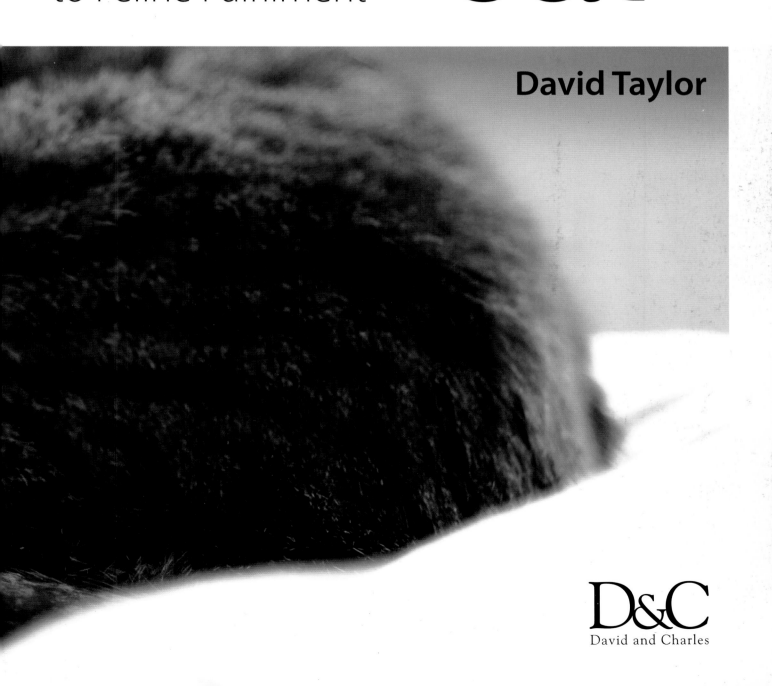

D&C
David and Charles

A DAVID & CHARLES BOOK
© F&W Media International Ltd 2011

David & Charles is an imprint of F&W Media
International, Ltd, Brunel House, Forde Close,
Newton Abbot, TQ12 4PU, UK

F&W Media International, Ltd is a subsidiary of F+W
Media, Inc., 4700 East Galbraith Road
Cincinnati OH45236, USA

First published in the UK in 2011

David Taylor has asserted his right to be identified as
author of this work in accordance with the Copyright,
Designs and Patents Act, 1988.

The publisher has endeavoured to contact all
contributors of text and/or pictures for permission to
reproduce. If there are any errors or omissions please
notify the publisher in writing.
A catalogue record for this book is available from the
British Library.

ISBN-13: 978-0-7153-3641-0
ISBN-10: 0-7153-3641-X

Printed in China RR Donnelley for:
F&W Media International, Ltd
Brunel House, Forde Close, Newton Abbot,
TQ12 4PU, UK

Produced for F&W Media International, Ltd by
SP Creative Design
Editor: Heather Thomas
Designer: Rolando Ugolini
Photographs: Gerard Brown and Rolando Ugolini;
iStockphoto: 22, 22, 23, 23, 23, 41, 59, 76, 77, 88, 88,
93, 111, 115, 127

Front cover image: © iStockphoto
Back cover images: © Rolando Ugolini (Top right),
(Bottom Left), (Bottom Middle).
© Gerard Brown (Bottom right).

For David & Charles
Senior Commissioning Editor: Freya Dangerfield
Senior Editor: Verity Muir
Senior Designer: Jodie Lystor
Senior Production Controller: Kelly Smith

F+W Media publishes high quality books on a wide
range of subjects
For more great book ideas visit:
www.rubooks.co.uk

Acknowledgements
The publishers would like to thank the following organizations
and individuals for their assistance in producing this book:
Wood Green Animal Shelters
Nicola Bacon, Rachel Radwell VN, Nicole Webster and Rhiannon Swann
Susan Mortimer and Alison Mackmin.

Contents

Introduction

Where does that cuddly fireside-loving feline companion of yours come from? About 65 to 70 million years ago, at the close of the age of the dinosaurs, the first mammals came on the scene – small, tree-climbing, long-nosed, insect-eating and intelligent.

The cat's ancestors

As the millennia passed, these primitive mammals took different pathways of development, some opting for a vegetarian diet as herbivores and others preferring a diet of meat. Among the carnivores were the earliest ancestors of the cat.

The first carnivorous mammals – creodonts – had long bodies, short legs and clawed feet. Although their brains were quite small, they were sufficiently developed to have 44 teeth for killing and chewing. The creodonts evolved into a whole range of predators, some of which were as big as wolves or lions. However, their relatively low intelligence led to a gradual decline, resulting in their extinction some 10,000,000 years ago. Luckily, before they died out, one of their forms gave rise to a new kind of animal: the miacid, which was a small, shy forest dweller with a much bigger brain.

As time passed, all the modern carnivores, including canids (dogs, wolves and foxes) and viverrids (mongooses, genets and civets) evolved from the miacids. It is probable that the cat family sprang from the ancient civet species.

Sacred pest controllers

Domesticated cats have had a relationship with human beings for thousands of years. It almost certainly began when agriculture replaced hunting as the most important part of the human economy in the Middle East. The African Wildcat, which is still common in all parts of Africa except waterless deserts and the depths of the equatorial forests, was attracted to the grain stores of ancient Egypt where food, in the form of rodents, could readily be found. These useful pest controllers probably began their duties around 3000BC.

In due course, the cats moved into the household and became loved as family pets. The Egyptians admired the strength, cunning and agility of these skilled hunters and started treating them as sacred. The name for these household gods was miw. Owners shaved off their eyebrows as a sign of mourning when their cat died and it was embalmed and mummified, placed in a wooden coffin and taken to the Great Temple of Bast, the cat god, at Bubastis.

Travelling cats

Cats were also domesticated in the Far East in ancient times. Whereas some experts date domestication in China at 2000BC, others place it as late as AD400. Longhaired cats probably have an ancestry originating from countries in the east. Modern Longhairs seem

Did you know?

There are records of cat shows in England as early as the sixteenth century but breeding for show purposes started in the late nineteenth century. In 1871, a show for Persian and British Shorthair types was held at London's Crystal Palace, and the first American cat show, for Maine Coons, was around the same time. New York's first big cat show was in Madison Square Garden on 8 May 1895. Some early cat shows had a ring class with cats on leads paraded en masse around a ring by their owners. You can imagine the scuffles that often occurred.

Did you know?

Sadly, the opportunity for scientists to study the vast numbers of feline mummies from Ancient Egypt was lost when, in 1889, nineteen tons of these mummies were shipped to Liverpool, England. Apart from one cat skull, which is now on show in the British Museum, the rest of this precious load was sold off – as fertilizer!

likely to be descended from the wild cats of Iran and Afghanistan, which, in turn, may have developed from the Manul, or Pallas's cat, that still inhabits those lands.

From Egypt, Phoenician traders took cats to Italy around 900BC, and from there they spread slowly across Europe. By the tenth century, domestic cats had arrived in England, although they were still rare.

The first colonists later took their cats with them to the New World, not least because of their skills in controlling rats on sailing vessels. Shorthaired cats arrived in the United States in the seventeenth century while Longhaired cats were imported into America from Britain in the late nineteenth century.

The development of breeds

Unlike dogs, cats have not been selectively bred over many centuries to perform a wide variety of specific tasks. Although they have been domesticated for thousands of years, the idea of producing pedigree pussies did not take hold until the mid-nineteenth century. The development of the many different breeds of domestic cat that we see today came about through cat lovers gradually selecting and cross-breeding individuals from the common or garden domestic types – 'street cats' if you will – that had been around for thousands of years. So, where once all cats were cross-breds resulting from accidental matings and natural selection, artificial selection by human beings gradually produced more than 100 cat breeds. We call them 'pedigrees', but in their genetic make-up they are all still, to some degree, 'mongrels'.

CHAPTER ONE

Acquiring your cat

A cat may be acquired after careful consideration and preparation on your part or accidentally, such as when one walks in off the street one day and decides to lodge with you, or you take one over after a relative or friend moves away or dies. Assuming you are in the position of being able to choose the pet yourself, here are some important things you'll have to think about.

Choosing a cat

Having decided that you want to welcome a cat into your home, you need to consider different aspects of your lifestyle and ask yourself some important questions.

Town or country

Do you live in a town or the country? Do you have a house – with or without a garden – or a flat in a multi-storey block? Some cats thrive on living in the country. These are robust, energetic types that relish the opportunity to hunt outside the house, and they are not suitable for folk living in high-rise apartments. Other cats, particularly many longhairs, are happy to live permanently indoors if they are provided with good litter facilities, and they fit in very well with an

elderly person living alone. Some cats can even be trained to walk successfully on a lead if the training begins when they are still quite young.

Family life

Do you live alone or within a family? Are there any young children in your household? Do you have any other family pets already? There are some cats that get on particularly well with children, dogs and other cats, and then there are the other ones that detest any form of competition.

Whereas some felines are solitary creatures living their own independent lives, others can be very demanding, vocal and loud, expecting abundant attention from their owners. Another issue to consider is whether there is anyone at home during the day or you all go out to work. If the latter is the case, then perhaps you should think about acquiring two cats, so that they keep one another company.

Time and lifestyle

Do you want an active, playful pet or simply a rather decorative 'salon' cat? Do you have the time and inclination to carry out the thorough daily grooming that longhaired cats must receive? Cats do not just take care of themselves and being a responsible owner is more than just putting some food down every day and changing a litter tray. A truly contented cat will need your care, attention and company. Like humans, however, they are all different, and they come with

◄ **Many cats enjoy city and suburban life, hunting in nearby parks and gardens, and often watching the world go by from a high vantage point, such as a tree or gate post.**

Did you know?

It is said that the cat flap was invented by the famous seventeenth-century mathematician and physicist Sir Isaac Newton.

▲ Many cats are quite happy to become fireside companions and spend most of the day inside the house, sleeping or stretching out in a sunny spot.

▼ Other cats prefer to be outside indulging in natural feline behaviours, such as stalking and hunting birds and small mammals.

their own personal preferences and eccentricities. For example, some cats love messing about with water or even swimming in it. I will deal with all these criteria later when describing the qualities and characteristics of the different breeds and types.

Allergies and sensitivity

If you or someone in your family is thought to be allergic to cats, perhaps you might consider obtaining one of the very shorthaired or even hairless pedigree breeds. It is a widely held belief that it is the hair of the cat's coat that triggers certain human allergic conditions, such as asthma. In fact, we now know that the cause is not the hair but rather a protein in the cat's saliva, which is deposited on the coat when it grooms itself. However, even very short-coated and hairless cats also groom themselves and leave traces of saliva on their skin, so they cannot be absolutely guaranteed not to trouble sensitive people.

Feline physical features

Unlike dogs, which come in a variety of shapes and sizes, domestic cats have not yet been produced with much in the way of anatomical extremes. The cat's body shows structural adaptations that suit its role as a quadruped, carnivorous predator. Its basics are the same as those of its wild hunting relatives: the tiger, lion and leopard.

Weight and flexibility

Adult cats generally weigh 2–5kg (6–12lb). The heaviest cat on record was a 13-year-old female tabby from Cumbria, England, tipping the scales at 18kg (40lb). The cat has a most elastic body. The spine is held together by muscles rather than ligaments, unlike humans, and this makes the back very flexible. The shoulder joint design permits the foreleg to be turned in almost any direction. Another factor that gives flexibility is that the cat has up to 26 more vertebrae than us. Also, unlike humans, it lacks a collarbone, having instead just a small scrap of clavicle tissue deep in the breast muscle. A full collarbone would broaden the chest and both reduce the cat's ability to squeeze through narrow spaces and limit the length of its stride.

Body shapes

There are three main body shapes in domestic cats: the cobby, the muscular and the lithe.
●The cobby cat is a solidly built animal with short, thick legs, broad shoulders and rump, and a short, rounded head with a flattish face. Examples include the various Longhairs/Persians.
●The muscular cat has medium-length legs, shoulders and rump, which are neither wide nor narrow, and a medium-length, slightly-rounded head. Examples of this type of cat include the British/European and American Shorthairs.
●The lithe cat is lightly built with long, slim legs, narrow shoulders and rump and a long, narrow, wedge-shaped head. The Siamese exemplifies this body shape.

▼ **The Persian's dense, long coat requires a lot of grooming and looking after to keep it in good condition.**

▲ The Korat is a short-haired breed that originated in Thailand. Although fearless, it dislikes noise.

▲ The Siamese is very inquisitive and extremely vocal. A one-person oriented cat, it craves human company.

▲ Persians are often kept as indoor cats but many are very active and enjoy being outside in the garden.

▲ The Birman is a very old breed from Burma, which was kept for many centuries as a Buddhist temple cat.

Coat types

The physical attractiveness of cats comes, along with their range of striking eye colours, from their coats. However, it is not just their beauty that you have to consider when you are deciding on a pet that carries a longhair, shorthair, semi-longhair or hairless coat – your time and lifestyle are important factors, too.

● Longhaired types must receive thorough, regular grooming, usually on a daily basis, if matting and the ingestion of furballs are to be avoided.

● Semi-longhaired cats also need to be groomed regularly. It is not true, as some folk often claim, that the fur of semi-longhairs, such as Birmans, does not tend to become matted.

● Shorthaired cats need less grooming, of course, but it still has to be done from time to time.

● Hairless cats, such as the Sphynx and Peterbald, lack a layer of furry insulation and must never be allowed to get cold – they should be carefully supervised if they go out of doors. They can also easily get sunburnt if they are exposed to too much sunlight.

Kinds of hair

Cats' coats are of several distinct types, and the nature of each is determined by the proportions of three different kinds of hair that make up the coat. These are the topcoat or guard hairs and two kinds of undercoat hairs – the bristly awn hairs and the soft, curly down hairs. Thus, for example, the full, dense coat of longhairs is composed of very long guard hairs coupled with plentiful long down hairs, but without any awn hairs.

Did you know?

Possibly the most expensive pedigree cat to date is the Bengal that was purchased by a woman in London in 1998 for $42,000.

▶ **Cats come in a wide range of coat colours and patterns, as shown here. They include tabbies (right and below far right), tortoiseshells (far right) and solid colours (below right).**

The coat of, say, the British Shorthair has quite short guard hairs, awn hairs that are short, sparse and only moderately curly, and no down hairs at all, whereas the American Wirehair cat possesses guard, awn and down hairs, all of which are short and very curly.

Colours and patterns

There is a complex vocabulary used to denote the wide variety of colours and patterns displayed by cats' coats. Here are some common terms.

● **Bi-colour:** A white coat with dark patches of any recognized colour.

● **Calico:** Also known as Tortoiseshell and White.

● **Cameo:** A white undercoat with tipped guard hairs of some recognized colour.

● **Chinchilla:** A pure white coat with black tipping.

● **Colourpoint:** A white, creamy or Ivory body with tail, paws, face and ears of another colour.

● **Dilute:** A pale shade of a colour.

● **Harlequin:** Black and white Bi-colour; also known as Piebald, Magpie or Tuxedo.

● **Mantle:** A dark topcoat above a pale undercoat.

● **Mitted (also known as 'Gloves'):** White paws on dark legs.

● **Part-colour:** Bi-colours and Tortoiseshells.

● **Points:** Coloured extremities: the ears, face, nose, paws and tail.

● **Self:** One single colour; also called Solid.

● **Shaded:** Medium tipping.

● **Shell:** Light tipping.

● **Silver:** White hairs with black or transparent tips that give a silvery effect.

● **Smoke:** A white undercoat with a topcoat that is white at the roots and coloured at the ends; darker points on back, head and feet.

● **Tabby:** This comes in four forms – Ticked (each hair has contrasting dark and light colour bands); Mackerel (vertically striped); Spotted (spots or blobs); and Classic (whorls or 'oyster' marks on the sides). All have a distinct 'M' mark on the forehead, 'spectacles' around the eyes, rings on the tail and 'broken rings' or bars on the legs.

● **Tipping:** The guard hairs of the overcoat are coloured along some of their length.

● **Torbie:** A mixture of Tabby and Tortoiseshell markings with white or cream.

● **Tortoiseshell (Tortie):** A two-coloured, black and red, coat.

● **Van pattern:** Largely white with patches of red or cream at the base of the ears and on the tail.

Pedigree or moggie?

Having set your heart on owning a cat, there are a number of decisions you need to make, such as whether you want a pedigree or non-pedigree. If you are interested in breeding or showing, buy a pedigree cat. Selecting a breed is a matter of personal taste, but remember that longhairs need thorough daily grooming and Siamese and Burmese can be demanding and vociferous and may mature more quickly than other cats. Non-pedigrees make enchanting pets and are equally rewarding as companions.

Pedigree cats, especially the recently developed so-called 'designer' breeds, are relatively expensive. However, you may be able to obtain a bargain, either by buying a 'pet-quality' cat that does not come up to the standards for showing but would nevertheless make a fine pet, or perhaps by making a breeding agreement, whereby you pay a reduced price for a show-quality cat and return it to the vendor at prearranged times for breeding purposes. If this is the case, the ownership of kittens must also be discussed in advance and whatever is agreed put into writing.

▼ **If you decide on a non-pedigree cat, you can allow it free access to roam and hunt outside in your garden.**

Which coat colour?

The chances are that you will have your own personal preferences when it comes to coat colours but do they matter? Well, some people think that the colour of a cat's coat can provide us with a valuable clue to its temperament and personality. Although not proven, tabbies are said to be good hunters, tortoiseshells are reputed to be fiery characters, and ginger cats are thought to be laid-back and gentle.

▲ **If you opt for a kitten rather than an adult cat, you must be prepared not only to house-train it but also to set aside some quality time each day for games and play.**

If your main objective is to have a cat purely as a companion, then why not opt for a non-pedigree? There are always lots of inexpensive cats of all coat colours and patterns that are in need of good homes. Contact your local animal rescue organization or humane society and go along, talk to the staff and select a cat that you immediately fall in love with or that clearly takes a fancy to you.

Neutering

Castrated toms and spayed queens make equally good and affectionate pets. Un-neutered toms spray strong-smelling urine, tend to go a-wandering and often get into fights with consequent wounds and infections. Un-neutered queens come into frequent heat (oestrus) at certain times of the year and, if you don't confine them indoors during these periods, they are likely to have unwanted pregnancies. Get your pet neutered.

▲ **A pedigree cat, such as this longhaired Persian, can be demanding on your time. The long coat will need thorough grooming every day to keep it in good condition.**

Kitten or adult?

Tiny, defenceless kittens are very attractive and appealing but they do require a lot of attention and house-training. However, on the plus side, they do adapt quicker than adults to their new environment. For many people, the best choice is to acquire a fully grown cat, particularly if they are out at work all day. If this is the case for you, consider getting two cats to provide companionship for each other. Solitary cats can become lonely and may develop bad habits.

Popular cat breeds

If you really prefer a pedigree pet to a moggie, there are over 100 breeds to choose from. To help you make an informed decision, here are some of the most popular characters with essential information on their temperament and care.

Longhairs

Persians/Longhairs

Most longhaired cats are of the exotic-looking Longhair type, which is popularly known as Persian. In the United States, the various colours and coat patterns are listed as varieties whereas in Britain they are called Longhairs with each colour classified as a separate breed. One of the rarest is the Black, while the Smoke Longhair/Persian has a particularly glamorous coat which shimmers when it moves. All these cats are very amenable, friendly and quintessential 'salon cats'. They make excellent companion pets, particularly for people who are living alone, and they are happy to spend most of their time indoors.

▼ **This Persian has a very glamorous, abundant coat which requires a lot of time and careful grooming.**

Ragdoll

The Ragdoll is one of the larger breeds of cat and is somewhat similar in appearance to the Birman (see opposite). When it is picked up, however, it is not at all Birman-like but relaxes all its muscles to become as weak as a kitten and as floppy as the doll from which it takes its name. It will lie draped over your arm like a waiter's napkin. Sweet natured and extremely tolerant of the whims and foibles of others, the Ragdoll quickly becomes devoted to its human owner. It likes company, whether human, feline or canine, and is good with children, dogs and other cats. Although it is fond of going outside, Ragdolls make first-class indoor pets and thrive in urban apartments. They need regular grooming although their coat tends not to matt.

▲ **Attractive and affectionate, the gentle Ragdoll loves to play games and makes a good all-round family pet.**

Maine Coon

The oldest American breed, this cat may have roamed free in the state of Maine in the early days of its history, drawing comparisons with the indigenous raccoon, which not only has a similar appearance to tabby-type Maine Coons but also similar hunting habits.

The severe New England climate contributed to the development of the Maine Coon's thick coat. Maine Coons come in all colours except Chocolate and Lilac points and Colourpoints. The most common variety is coppery brown marked in black.

This is a most friendly, companionable cat with two characteristic behaviours: it loves to 'sleep rough', curling up in the oddest positions in the strangest places, and it 'talks' with a charming, quiet, chirping sound. Maine Coons need plenty of space – either in the country, where they can roam around, or in town, where they are happy to live indoors but should be provided with an outdoor pen.

Semi-longhairs

Birmans

This 'sacred cat of Burma' adapts well to family life and gets on with other animals as well as humans. The breed comes in several varieties depending on the colour of the points, including Seal-point, Blue-point, Chocolate-point and Lilac-point. Birmans are generally happy to spend most of their time indoors. Placid and

▲ **One of the largest breeds of cat, the Maine Coon has a dense, shaggy coat which can resemble that of a racoon.**

laid-back temperamentally, they nevertheless crave attention and their semi-longhaired coats must be brushed and combed regularly to avoid matting.

▼ **With its sapphire blue eyes and distinctive points, the Birman is a very beautiful cat.**

Shorthairs

There are distinct British, European and American Shorthaired breeds with numerous colour varieties. Easy-going, placid and intelligent, British and European Shorthairs make affectionate pets. American Shorthairs are more independent by nature but also excellent companions. They tend not to be very vocal, often mouthing silent miaows. Some Oriental shorthaired breeds, notably the popular and elegant Siamese, are incredibly demanding – their vocalizations are imperious, loud and impossible to ignore. The Siamese is a highly intelligent cat and usually becomes devoted to its owner – sometimes to the extent that it may not tolerate any 'rivals' to his or her affections.

▶ **The British Shorthair is one of the most popular breeds in the UK today.**

▶ **The Siamese is vocal and very inquisitive. It makes an affectionate but demanding pet.**

Rex cats

These cats have distinctive short, tightly-curled coats. The three breeds – Devon, Cornish and German Rex – are available in a variety of coat and eye colours. They are all very affectionate, sociable, playful and well disposed towards other animals. A fourth Rex breed,

the Selkirk Rex, was developed in the United States in the late 1980s. Its coat curls vary in tightness but they are usually looser and more wavy than those of the other Rex breeds.

▲ **The Siamese is slender, elegant and long-limbed.**

Manx

Legend has it that the Manx cat lost its tail when Noah closed the door to his ark a little too hastily. An ideal family cat, the Manx has a placid, good-natured temperament. It emits a pleasant 'trilling' sound when talking to kittens or its owner. It is a good jumper and climber, and in its enthusiasm for chasing, retrieving and burying toys it is positively dog-like!

▲ **The distinctive Manx breed of cat has no tail.**

Snowshoe

Also known as 'Silver Laces', this popular American breed combines the beauty of the Siamese with American Shorthair bulk. With its sparkling, 'bomb-proof' personality, this lively, active and athletic cat delights in running, leaping and chasing toys and particularly relishes interactive games. Generally, a Snowshoe enjoys being around water and may even like swimming. It prefers to have company most of the time, loves being petted, and is excellent with children, other cats and dogs. Compared to the Siamese, it is more laid-back and less noisy and makes an ideal indoor pet. However, it does require lots of attention and sufficient space and facilities to expend its boundless energy. It does not appreciate being left alone for long periods, so in households where family members are out at work all day, it is best to have another cat to keep it company.

Russian Blue

This elegant and graceful cat is a sweet-natured, quiet and reserved character. Indeed, queens can be so quiet that it may be difficult to tell when they are calling in oestrus (heat). Russian Blues don't tend to go a-wandering and seem to prefer the indoor life. They get on well with children, other cats and dogs but do not like excessive handling or being teased. Loving and loyal, they are one of the feline breeds that is most amenable to being lead-trained. Russian Blues tend to be greedy eaters and they are prone to obesity if their diet is not carefully controlled.

▲ **The graceful Russian Blue.**

Bengal

The unusual and very distinctive Bengal resembles a miniature wild cat with its spotted, banded coat. Originally bred by mating the Asian Leopard Cat with a domestic shorthair, this breed is becoming increasingly popular. Although its ancestry is recently part-wild, it is loving and playful and settles down well to family life. However, Bengals are natural hunters and do not make good house cats – they need plenty of space and the freedom to roam, albeit under their owner's supervision in an enclosed garden or even an outside run. The short coat is thick with a luminous sheen and requires only minimal grooming. Bengals may be either

▲ **Owning a Bengal is like having a wild cat in your home.**

Snow coloured with a pearly sheen, or predominantly black and brown with a gold dusting. The soft fur under the body is paler, the legs are barred and the tail has a dark tip. The eyes are usually green but may be gold, hazel or blue.

Burmese

This elegant cat has a glossy, short coat with a satin finish. There is a wide range of coat colours, including several Tortoiseshells. The number of varieties of Burmese differs on each side of the Atlantic. The American Burmese also has a rounder body, head, eyes and feet than the British cat. These cats are famous as people-lovers. Intelligent and highly affectionate, they make superb pets, but they can also be quite demanding, pestering their owners to get what they want – and they don't like being teased.

▼ **The elegant Burmese.**

Finding a cat

One of the best ways to find your new cat is to ask your vet about local breeders and rescue organizations. They will be able to recommend the best route for you, depending on whether you want a pedigree or a moggie, a kitten or an adult.

Pedigree cats

If you decide that you want a pedigree cat, your best source is a specialist breeder, although this will probably be the most expensive option. To find a responsible breeder, you can contact your local cat club for a list of names and addresses of breeders in your area or visit a cat show and meet a number of breeders. Many breeders also have websites on the internet. The prize-winning potential of a cat can only be gauged by an expert eye, so if you plan to show your cat or use it for breeding, when you go to inspect a possible feline purchase, always take along someone who is familiar with the breed in question and who understands exactly what you hope for from the cat. When choosing a pedigree kitten, it is best to see a whole litter with their mother in the breeder's home. There you will be able to observe the conditions under which they have been raised and see how they animals behave and interact with each other. You can also check the temperament and health of the mother.

Did you know?

BREEDING AGREEMENTS
If you cannot afford the full price of a pedigree animal, you could try to get a 'bargain' by buying a 'pet-quality' cat or making a breeding agreement. 'Pet-quality' animals may not quite match the standards required for showing, but nevertheless they do make good pets. Under a breeding agreement, you buy a show-quality cat and return it to the vendor at prearranged times for breeding. Discuss who will own the kittens and put whatever is agreed in writing.

Cross-breeds and moggies

If your main objective in owning a cat is for it to be your companion, there are always plenty of inexpensive cross-bred animals and moggies of indeterminate pedigree in need of homes. Humane societies and charitable cat rescue organizations require loving owners for thousands of abandoned cats. Cheaper than pedigree cats, these moggies make good pets and can be integrated into families as loyal, affectionate companions. The staff at the rescue centre will have some background information about the cats in their care and their individual temperaments and health. This helps them to match the wishes of potential owners to the needs of the cats that need rehoming. Don't be offended if they ask you a lot of personal questions about your home and lifestyle and check that you know how to look after a cat properly before handing it over.

Pet shops

If you have a choice, do not buy a cat or kitten, however cute or appealing it may look, from a pet shop. Young cats, in particular, are very susceptible to diseases, which spread easily in pet shop conditions. In addition, it is highly unlikely that they have been adequately socialized, which may cause common behavioural problems, such as indoor spraying and even aggression to people and other cats.

▼ **You need to decide whether you want a pedigree, cross-breed or moggie before you start looking for your new pet. Moggies make loving and good companions.**

◀ The cats awaiting rehoming in the rescue centre look appealing and defenceless. Find out about their history and health before selecting one to take home.

Choosing a kitten

When choosing a cat, the attraction of a tiny, defenceless kitten is obvious, but it will demand lots of your attention in the early months and will need to be house-trained. You cannot just take a kitten home and expect it to look after itself. On the plus side, a kitten will normally adapt quickly to its new environment, but if you are out at work all day or think that a kitten might be too boisterous or difficult to train, a fully grown adult cat would be a better choice for your lifestyle and circumstances.

The right kitten for you

As mentioned earlier, it is wisest to inspect a kitten, along with its littermates, at the breeder's home. When selecting a kitten, it is better to go for one that is bigger, bolder, playful and inquisitive rather than the smallest, most retiring member of the litter. If you want a quiet, contented pet, look for a calm kitten with an even personality that does not mind being handled. Whatever kind of cat you want, and no matter where you obtain it, there is one golden rule: always make a careful study of the animal's condition and state of health. Never take on a cat that is sickly, no matter how convincing the vendor's excuses may be. If your request to examine the cat yourself is rejected, don't buy it. Any responsible vendor will understand that it is reasonable to check a new pet thoroughly.

▼**Sometimes it is a good idea to take two kittens instead of one, as they are company for each other and will play happily together when you are busy working.**

Assessing a kitten

Before inspecting a kitten, always wash your hands thoroughly and play with the animal a little to help put it at ease. Then grasp the body firmly but gently and begin your examination.

1 Feel the texture of the kitten's coat. It should be smooth and free from any matts. Look for the telltale signs of fleas – the droppings will resemble tiny specks of black coal dust in the fur.
2 Are the kitten's ears clean, sweet-smelling and dry without any accumulations of wax?
3 Check that the eyes are clean and bright without any protrusion of the third eyelids.
4 The nose should be damp but free from any discharge.
5 A healthy kitten should have a pink mouth and white teeth without any inflammation of the gums.

6 Lift the tail and look for any signs of diarrhoea – the anal area should be clean.

7 Gently feel under the abdomen with one hand. It should be slightly rounded, but not hard. Make sure there are no lumps (possible evidence of a hernia).

8 Finally, let the kitten move around freely, so you can look for signs of lameness.

Veterinary inspection

A veterinary examination before you purchase is ideal. Indeed, if you are buying an expensive pedigree cat, it is essential. Ask your own vet to perform it, and to provide a written certificate of health. Where a kitten is obtained from a humane society, a veterinary inspection is usually carried out before the animal is handed over. Nevertheless, wherever you obtain your cat, make an appointment for your vet to check it over as soon as possible after acquisition. Make sure that the kitten has been vaccinated against feline influenza, feline panleucopenia (feline enteritis) and feline leukaemia at least one week before purchase.

Proof of vaccination must be provided in the form of a written veterinary certificate. All pedigree animals should be registered under an individual name, along with details of their colour and parents, when they are about five weeks old. Unless this is done, they cannot enter a cat show in a pedigree class.

Sexing a kitten

Differentiating between male and female kittens is not always very easy. Lift the tail and look at the opening beneath the anus.

• A female kitten can be distinguished by the closeness of her vulva to the anus, and the two openings may appear to be joined together.

• In the case of a male kitten, there is a raised dark area beneath the anus, which will develop into testicles, and below this, the penis.

◄ **Whether you want to acquire a kitten or an adult cat, do examine it first. Pay special attention to the mouth, ears and eyes for clues to health problems.**

Choosing an adult cat

If you decide that you want to rehome an adult cat, whether it's from a rescue centre, a breeder or even a friend or relative who can no longer keep it (for example, when they move away from the area, get divorced or someone dies), there are several important issues to be considered before you take your new pet home.

Neutering

In my opinion, there is nothing to choose between a castrated tom and a spayed queen; both make equally good, affectionate pets. An un-neutered tom is not advisable, however, as it will spray pungent urine, frequently wander and possibly get into fights with consequent wounds and infections. An un-neutered queen should be avoided for similar reasons: she will have frequent heat periods (oestrus) at certain times of the year, and, if you don't confine her indoors on those occasions she may well have unwanted pregnancies. Neutering eliminates these disadvantages and may make the cat more affectionate. If the cat is an adult that has not been neutered, the operation of castration or spaying can still be done, whatever its age. Neutering operations performed under general anaesthetic by a veterinarian are completely humane.

Did you know?

FERAL CATS

Do not be tempted to take on a feral cat unless you are a very experienced cat owner with a lot of patience. Because they have grown up in the wild and have never been socialized, they shy away from humans and are extremely difficult to domesticate. Many ferals will only tolerate humans in order to obtain food.

▲ Talk to the staff and get to know and handle the cats at the rescue centre before making your final selection.

Rescuing a cat

When you go to the rescue centre or humane society, talk to the staff. Explain your circumstances, your working hours and lifestyle, where you live, whether you have other pets and how these might affect bringing a new cat into your household.

When they show you the available cats, don't be afraid to ask them questions about their background, why they are in rescue and whether they have been badly treated. Find out if anything is known about their past health: have they been checked over by a vet, been neutered and vaccinated – if so, are there certificates to prove this? Ask about their dietary preferences and temperament, whether they have any behavioural problems and how they get on with other cats.

When you see a cat you like, introduce yourself and try handling it gently to see how it responds to you. For example, is it friendly and outgoing or suspicious and defensive? Whereas an extrovert, sociable cat will not object to being picked up and stroked, a nervous cat may wriggle or run for a bolt-hole.

When you handle the cat, check it over physically (see page 26), looking for any signs of ill health. If you suspect that there is something wrong with it, don't take it, however appealing and friendly the animal – just harden your heart and walk away. Once you have decided on a particular Puss, if there is no set fee, please do leave at least a small donation in cash for the rescue centre; they need it and deserve it.

▶ **Some rescue cats may be fearful or timid and may try to escape or struggle as you handle them. Remember that they may be stressed and find it difficult to relax.**

Feline personalities

What sort of cat do you want – an adventurous, playful extrovert, a quiet, independent loner or a more timid introvert? Would you like a free-roaming moggie or a house cat that is kept permanently indoors? When you acquire an adult cat, choose the right cat for your temperament and circumstances, so that you end up with a contented, home-loving pet.

Planning ahead

You cannot simply dash off, find a cat or kitten you fancy and then bring it home without making some important preparations beforehand for the new family member. You will not only need to invest in some cat-friendly equipment but may also have to make certain safety modifications to your home and garden.

Carrying container

First of all, you will need some form of secure carrying container to collect your new cat and to transport it to the vet. This may be a smart plastic travelling case, an old-fashioned basketwear container or even a temporary cardboard carrying box.

Cat bed

A snug cat bed is essential. A wide range of designs is available in pet shops, including my favourite – a hammock that hangs over a radiator. Be sure to pick a bed that will be big enough for your curled-up cat. Equip it with a soft, snug lining such as a cushion or, best of all, a piece of sheepskin. The bed should be placed in some quiet spot out of the main flow of human traffic. Cats being cats, your kitten or new adult cat may decide to change its preferred slumbering spot when it settles in and becomes familiar with its new surroundings.

▼ **Your cat will need a cosy bed to curl up in and sleep. After the initial exploration, it will soon settle down. Place the bed in a peaceful, quiet, out-of-the-way spot.**

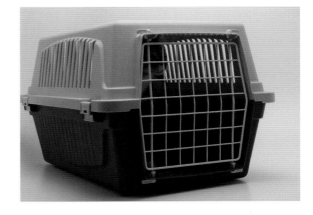

▲ **A sturdy plastic travelling case is a good investment and will last for many years. Put a soft blanket or some sheepskin in the base to make it more comfortable.**

Litter tray

Even if, in due course, you intend to teach your kitten or cat how to use a cat flap, so that it can go outdoors, you will need a litter tray, which it will choose to use when the weather is bad outside. This should be positioned in a quiet area of your home, out of the way of household traffic, where your pet will be able to go about its private affairs undisturbed with dignity.

▲ **All cats can learn to use a litter tray, no matter what their age. It is essential for house cats that live indoors.**

Bowls, grooming tools and ID

Other items you must obtain ahead of the new arrival are food and water bowls, which can be easily cleaned separately from the family crockery, and grooming tools in the form of a soft brush or hand-glove brush and a fine-toothed comb. Even if the cat or kitten has been micro-chipped you would still be well advised to fit it with a collar and identification disc.

Scratching post and toys

You may also want to consider getting a scratching post, pad or pyramid, a climbing frame or playpen, and a selection of cat toys. If the cat will not have access to a garden outside, provide a box in which you grow seedling grass and maybe some cereal grass, sage, thyme or – the big favourite – catmint.

Pet insurance

Taking out pet insurance for your new arrival is always sensible. With any luck, your cat will stay hale and hearty for many years to come, but if it does fall ill

Did you know?

Cats use their whiskers to gain important information from the world around them. They act as wind detectors, enabling the animal to pinpoint the direction from which any particular odour is coming. Loss of its whiskers weakens a kitten's sense of orientation in its surroundings, which is why a mother cat will bite off the whiskers of kittens that stray too far away!

or have an accident, veterinary treatment can be very expensive. There are several good pet insurance schemes on the market. Ask your vet or breeder to recommend one, or explore the different options available on the internet.

▲ **An indoor scratching post will keep your cat's claws in good condition and provide a sensible alternative to scratching your cherished furniture.**

▼ **Cats enjoy using a scratching post. Hanging a colourful toy from it will help to make it more attractive to your pet.**

Making your home safe

Cats do sometimes get into trouble while they are in the house or garden. As a responsible owner, you should check your home for possible problem areas in case there are potential hazards for a young, inquisitive creature that might well have a penchant for chewing, licking and generally investigating things. Do this before your new pet's arrival and from time to time thereafter.

Quick checklist

Some of the most important points to consider in your home and garden are the following:

- If you have an open fire, is there a protective fireguard and is access to the chimney blocked?
- Are all electric cables inaccessible to a chew-happy cat or disconnected when not in use?
- Are there any valued or valuable objects, such as ornaments, within reach of an agile and inquisitive cat?
- Do you have guards for hotplates and hobs?
- Are all your rubbish bins inaccessible?

- Are your doors and windows secure to stop a house cat escaping or to prevent potential falls from upper floors and balconies?
- Keep all sharp utensils, kitchen knives, small objects and plastic bags where the cat cannot reach them.
- Keep the oven, refrigerator, freezer, washing machine and dishwasher doors closed at all times.
- Keep all the cupboard and wardrobe doors shut to prevent a cat getting trapped inside.
- Keep garden ponds securely netted or install a low fence around them.

▼ **Trailing electric cables can be dangerous. Never leave them hanging down and always unplug kettles and other electric appliances when they are not being used.**

Feline essentials

POISONOUS PLANTS

Certain plants of both the indoor and garden varieties are poisonous for cats that chew them. Do not allow your pet access to the following: Elephant's Ears, Clematis, Dumb Cane, Fuchsia, Poinsettia, True Ivy, Laburnum, Sweet Pea, Mistletoe, Oleander, Philodendron, Laurel, Cherry Laurel, Rhododendron, Azalea, False Jerusalem Cherry and Winter Cherry.

TOXIC CHEMICALS

Many chemicals are frequently stored in the home or garden sheds and your cat must be denied access to them. They should be locked away securely out of reach. Chemicals to watch out for include the following: rodent poisons, arsenical horticultural sprays, insecticides, tar products, phenols, cresols, turpentine, aspirin, detergents, household cleaning solutions and automobile antifreeze.

◀ Take care when leaving breakable items and liquids unattended. Cats can jump on to tables and high surfaces.

◀ If you have a house cat, keep windows closed to prevent it escaping to the great outdoors. Windows on upper floors should be kept shut for obvious safety reasons.

Collecting your new cat

So the big day has arrived at last and you are off to collect your new feline companion. However, you will need to prepare yourself for the journey, even if it is only a very short one, by getting organized and making a few simple plans before you set out.

Heading home

Before you set out, make sure that you have a secure carrying container for your new pet. This can be a custom-made plastic or basketwear carrier or even a cheaper temporary cardboard container. They are all available from good pet stores. Put some newspaper or an old towel in the base of the container to make the cat comfortable and in case of accidents.

It is best if two of you go; one person to drive and the other to hold the cat box on their knees. If the journey is a long one, make sure that you take a bottle of water and a bowl or saucer with you, so that the cat or kitten can be given a drink from time to time. Before you put the cat or kitten in the container in preparation for returning home, check it all over for any signs of abnormality. Is it alert and mobile? Are the ears and nose clean and clear? Is the coat intact without any bald or rough patches? Lift up the tail to check that there is no soiling that might indicate diarrhoea. If you have any doubts at all, ask the breeder or members of staff at the rescue centre and perhaps pop into the vet's surgery on the way home.

If you are collecting a kitten and it has already been vaccinated, you should be given the vaccination papers. If it is a pedigree, you should also receive its pedigree papers. Find out what sort of food it has been eating and, if possible, take some of it home with you. Now you are ready! Put your new kitten or cat in the carrier by picking it up gently but firmly, supporting its bottom with one hand. Close the carrier door quickly and fasten it securely.

Settling in

Introducing your cat or kitten to its new household is a process that must not be rushed. When you get home, put it in a quiet room with its litter tray, some tasty food

▶ **To make the travel crate more cosy, and in case of mishaps, line the base with an old towel. Carry it smoothly and carefully without any jerky movements.**

▲ **Give your new cat the opportunity and time to explore his surroundings and settle in to his new home.**

▶ **Get your new cat accustomed to being handled right from the start. Only do this for short periods, however, and don't over-fuss him if he wants to jump down.**

and a bowl of water, and do not let it out for at least 24 hours. During this time you should visit it frequently, talking to and making a fuss of it.

Do not introduce other family members until your cat is relating confidently to you. When eventually they can be allowed in, ask them to wait until it approaches them. Children, in particular, need careful supervision. No kitten or even an adult cat relishes being rushed at by a happily screeching child. Nor should you pick your cat up at every opportunity. Talk to it, use some of its new cat toys to play simple games with it and, as its confidence grows, reward it with some tasty small food treats and lots of lavish praise.

Introducing other pets

If there are already some other pets in your household, they can be introduced to the newcomer after the first day or so – but only in strictly controlled conditions. Ask another family member to bring the resident pet into the room where you are sitting, holding the new cat or kitten securely in your arms. Make sure that you carefully control the encounter and have some tasty

food treats at hand to reward good behaviour by any of the animals. It is very important that you are seen to be even-handed in giving your affection to both the new cat or kitten and the established residents.

Other cats can sometimes show antipathy towards a newcomer in their midst and, unfortunately, this can continue for a few days or even over a longer period of several weeks. The early encounters between your pets should not last for too long during the first few days. Over-boisterous dogs, in particular, should be distracted by offering them small food treats and then separated from the cat. A persistently aggressive dog is best muzzled during the first few meetings and then trained gradually to be gentle and accept the cat by a system of rewards. Be patient and do not try to rush this process – it may take some time.

Did you know?

Cats purr, of course, when they are happy, but they can also produce a special purr that contains a hidden high-pitched tone – one that triggers a sense of urgency in the human brain. This is the purr the cat uses whenever he wants something specific from his owner – typically some food or a tasty titbit!

Using a cat flap

It is a relatively simple procedure to train your cat or kitten to use a cat flap. Using a favourite treat or toy, encourage it to come in rather than go out through the flap, which you can prop or wedge open. Then, over time, gradually lower the flap. The cat or kitten will soon learn what is required of it, usually within a week.

The first few days

You and your new arrival are beginning the process of getting to know one another and forming a relationship. Cats are naturally inquisitive – 'nosey' might be a more apt description – and your pet will explore and investigate its new home and surroundings incessantly. It may even get under your feet as it goes about its business.

Peace and quiet

Most cats sleep on average for 16 hours out of 24. They apparently need all that napping and you should leave them alone to just get on with it. Don't try to play with, handle or stimulate your cat excessively – let it decide when it wants to be active.

Allowing your cat some space is particularly important if there is a resident dog in your household. Don't get impatient with their attitude towards one another – be prepared for the fact that mutual acceptance may take many weeks. However, you must ensure that there are adequate sanctuaries and escape routes in the house that are always available to the cat. Its main sleeping place – its basket or cradle – should be located where the dog cannot interfere with it. Similarly, the litter tray and feeding bowls should be located out of the dog's reach. Cats generally prefer to be elevated and they may feel more secure if they are fed on a shelf or even on top of a cupboard.

Guidelines for mutual harmony

Feed your dog separately and alone – trouble can easily arise if a cat decides to filch some of the dog's dinner. Keep the dog's lead attached to its collar at all times, including those times when it is inside the house. This allows you to grab and restrain the dog if it suddenly threatens the cat.

Do not start cat-flap training immediately but rather keep it locked until both your dog and cat have come to tolerate one another more or less amicably. Otherwise your cat may nip out – perhaps for good! Most importantly, when all family members are away from the house, leave the cat and the dog in separate rooms until they really have reached an understanding and get on well together.

Outside exploration

Your cat's initial explorations of your garden or back yard should always be supervised by a family member. The neighbourhood cat fraternity may well consider

Feline essentials

Cats are very clean animals by nature and toilet training is relatively simple, especially when a kitten has been brought up by its natural mother. With fostered kittens, their instinct to cover their faeces means that most will readily adopt the litter tray. Covered litter trays are ideal for nervous cats or those who like privacy.

Did you know?

Arguably the most expert mouse-hunting cat in history was 'Mickey' of Burscough, Lancashire, who killed over 22,000 mice in 23 years.

your property to be their territory, and your walls or fences their walkways and observation posts. Your new pet is, therefore, an outsider who is encroaching upon their traditional domain.

As we shall see later on in this book, cats have their own society with complex relationships and hierarchies. Your cat, depending on its sex, age and temperament, will, if it goes out of doors regularly, gradually be absorbed into some position, high or low, within the local feline mafia. Until that happens, and often even afterwards, you may have frequent visits from some macho tom who is intent on staking a claim by spraying pungent urine on your doorstep, window sills or cat flap.

▶ Give your new cat plenty of time to settle into its new home. Everything will be unfamiliar and it should not be exposed to too much too soon.

▼ Even adult rescue cats will eventually relax in their new surroundings and make themselves thoroughly at home, even if it's on your bed.

Visiting the vet

It is a sensible idea to ring your local veterinary clinic and book your new cat in as soon as possible for a thorough examination. Hopefully, it will not need medical attention too often during its lifetime, but it is good for the cat to become acquainted with its doctor at an early stage and to get accustomed to visiting the clinic.

The first appointment

If possible, find a vet in your area who specializes in treating cats. Nowadays, few vets visit their feline patients in their own homes, and when they do, it is relatively expensive. Taking your pet to the surgery may possibly expose it to other infectious diseases carried by animals in the waiting room, so, on the appointed day, try to arrange a fixed appointment and then keep your cat in its basket or travelling container in your car until you are called in.

▼ **Let your cat explore and get used to its new travelling crate. Line the base with a soft rug and put a tasty titbit inside to tempt it to enter.**

Vaccinations

Your new cat may have already been vaccinated against the important infectious feline diseases and have the certificates to prove it. If not, make sure that you keep it indoors until it has been vaccinated and discuss with your vet the most appropriate time to take it to the surgery for vaccination. In most cases, the 'starter' vaccination course consists of two injections given three to four weeks apart, with the first one administered at eight or nine weeks of age. After that, the cat will require a booster dose of vaccine once a year, although, in recent years, many veterinarians have come to the opinion that this is unnecessary, so ask your vet what is advisable.

▲ **Always cover your cat's travelling crate with a blanket or towel to make it feel more secure and shield it from the cold when carrying the crate.**

It is important that all cats, including rescue cats and strays if you do not know whether they have been vaccinated, should get 'shots' against feline influenza and feline enteritis (panleucopenia).

Neutering and parasites

Neutering (castration of a male or spaying of a female) is an important issue to discuss with your vet if it has not already been carried out. Neutering prevents unwanted pregnancies as well as unsociable behaviour, such as spraying and wandering, in males – it is not cruel. Toms should be castrated after they are nine months old; queens can be spayed when they are four to nine months of age.

Your vet will also advise you on treating your pet for common parasites, such as tapeworms, hookworms, roundworms and whipworms. Safe and effective deworming drugs for oral dosing, either directly into

▶ **You can use a special flea comb to remove any fleas. Although it is quite effective, it is not fool-proof, so apply some anti-flea medication, too.**

Lice, ticks and mites

Apart from fleas, other skin parasites can bother your cat, including two kinds of louse: a sucking and a biting type. The most common site is on the head, but they can lodge anywhere. A heavily infested cat will be run-down and anaemic. Country-dwelling cats can pick up sheep ticks which suck blood and swell to resemble blackcurrants. As their mouthparts are buried securely in the cat's skin, you mustn't pull them off as the mouthpart may be left behind, causing an abscess. Apply a drop of chloroform or ether to them, wait until the mouthparts relax and then pick them off with tweezers.

Mange mites can burrow into a cat's skin, causing chronic inflammation, hair loss and irritation. The commonest species affects the head and ear area. Other mites are the autumn harvest mite and fur mite. Consult your vet for an appropriate treatment.

the mouth or mixed with food, can be prescribed and you will be given a schedule for administering these products on a regular basis. Preventive treatment is preferable to tackling worms after they attack.

Also, talk to your vet about avoiding your cat becoming infested with those unpleasant skin parasites – fleas. There are many different types of anti-flea preparations available (see page 130).

see also...

Health checks
pages 104–105

Flea treatments
page 130

Vaccinations
pages 134–135

CHAPTER TWO

How cats think

Cats' thinking is reactive, a response to stimuli received from the world around them. In a stimulus-free environment, their brain activity shuts down, unlike that of human beings who think proactively, pondering, wondering and creating thoughts. Cats, however, do not compose poetry nor do they just sit and think. Their thinking and intelligence depend upon the information that is provided by a range of highly-tuned senses, some of which are far more sophisticated than ours.

Cat behaviour

In essence, the cat is one of nature's most perfectly designed animals. It is a design that works supremely well – it looks good, functions precisely, owes nothing to anyone, gives much and demands little. Ever aware, it is always finely 'tuned in', via its array of highly developed senses, to the surrounding world.

Family tree

The domestic cat has a family tree containing the most cunning, subtle, dangerous and brave mammals on the planet. Of course, your pet is more docile than a puma or leopard, but unlike other domesticated animals, such as the dog, it has an independent streak that leads back to its wild past. The cat was tamed by Man much later than other domestic beasts and its inclination is never to fawn or creep. If you want an obedient servant as a pet, it would be wiser to pick a dog instead.

Natural hunters

Although dogs and cats are both classical carnivores, the cat is more adapted to the role of hunter. Wild dogs hunt in packs while cats, with the exception of some lion prides, seek out their prey singly. Like its wild cousins, the cat walks alone, and this individuality makes it a particularly suitable pet for the individualistic sort of human being.

Did you know?

If trouble is brewing – say, the cross-eyed tom from next door comes a-lurking – a queen will suddenly growl an alarm call and all her kittens will scatter and hide while she deals with the unwanted visitor. They will remain motionless until the alarm is over. Cubs of wild species, such as the Bobcat, act similarly when danger threatens. A Black-footed Cat queen even emits an 'all clear' call when the coast is clear.

▼ **Outdoor cats enjoy prowling and hunting, whether going for a stroll in the garden during the day or stalking their prey at dawn or dusk. The motivation to hunt is a natural instinct, which has nothing to do with hunger.**

The physical anatomy, behavioural characteristics and spirit of domestic cats, be they ordinary moggies, longhaired Persians or svelte Siamese, closely resemble those of their wild forbears and living wild relatives. Just beneath the skin of your slumbering fireside ginger tom, the ocelot elegantly reclines, and in the face of your tabby queen gazing intently at the sparrow newly landed on your lawn, you can see the unblinking eye of the tiger lying in ambush.

The feline hunting technique is a marvel of stealth and subtlety. In the domestic pet cat, hunting is not necessarily related to hunger – rather, it is a kind of sport or game, which, crucially, keeps all the warrior cat's skills well polished.

On watch

As a hunter, your pet has sharp eyesight and much of the day is spent in keen observation of the world. If it is in 'active mode', purposefully hunting prey, it will lurk in places where it cannot be seen – behind bushes, half-open doors or in long grass. However, if it is on 'auto-pilot', taking one of its frequent naps, it will choose a vantage point where it is safe from attack: outdoors, this is often high up on something such as a tree; indoors, where it feels more secure, it may choose a chair or bed. Even when it is dozing, it is still receiving messages through its senses and is able to spring into action at the slightest hint of danger. We can say therefore that the cat is at all times 'on watch' and ready to defend its territory against intruders.

▲ **Your cat's body language can tell you a lot about its behaviour and what it is thinking. Note the position of the ears and tail especially – these will give you clues.**

▼ **This cat is very focused and intent on watching something. Cats can sit quietly and patiently waiting before pouncing on their prey or a toy.**

A day in the life

What does the average cat, in particular one that is allowed to go outside, get up to during the day? Most owners don't know what their cats do. Learning more about your pet's haunts and habits, however, can help you to understand the animal and its behaviour and will surely keep both of you more contented.

Early risers

Cats are crepuscular by nature, tending to be out and about in the twilight hours of dawn and dusk. They can easily be trained to sleep during the eight hours their owners spend in slumber, but they need much more snooze-time over 24 hours than that. If you leave food down overnight, your cat will do most of his eating between the hours of 4am and 8am.

Time to stand and stare

After the first meal of the day, cats usually retire again for a morning nap, which can last until mid-afternoon and is undertaken in a desirable spot, sun-warmed in summer and fire or radiator-warmed in winter. On waking, they usually look for more nourishment before going out for a stroll. They do not go in for strenuous exercise but keep in good condition just by stretching their muscles occasionally. A cat does no physical work but spends much of its time looking, observing and contemplating.

Do cats dream?

Yes, electro-encephalographic studies have shown that they do. Dreaming can often be accompanied by external signs – movements of paws and claws and frequently emitted regular chirping, humming or buzzing sounds.

Promenading and socializing

Once outside, the cat takes a leisurely walk round the garden or yard. If there is a goldfish pond it might go there and weigh up its chances. The domestic cat is the only member of the genus *Felis* that eats fish and it is quite adept at hooking them out of shallow water.

The cat may pause to munch some blades of grass. Chewing grass is not, as often supposed, a sign that a cat is unwell. It is good for cats, containing useful vitamins and acting as an emetic, helping the animal regurgitate unwanted ingested matter, such as furballs.

As the cat continues, it may meet another feline, approaching it quite slowly in cautious but friendly mode with his tail held high in a greeting posture, while the other cat stands motionless, adopting a similar attitude. With heads and necks extended and crouching slightly, the cats investigate and sniff each other. Our cat's sense of smell reports that the stranger is a non-threatening, neutered tom. Next they obtain more chemical information by sniffing delicately along each other's neck, flank and, finally, bottom. Each cat wants to sniff the other's bottom first before allowing its own fundament to be checked out. If neither is prepared to be sniffed first, trouble may arise and fighting could erupt.

When bumping into a human being, a friendly cat will usually utter a cry of greeting. The voice is not strident or imploring but may be muted and diffident in a shy cat. Suspicious, particularly feral, cats will not greet you in this way but, after halting briefly to weigh you up, will run away at speed.

Patrolling the neighbourhood

The cat may venture out beyond the garden, checking out scent marks left by neighbourhood cats. It can tell if the scent is new or old and whether the depositor may still be close by. The cat's swivelling ears pick up the faintest rustling sounds in a patch of sun-dried grass and his stereophonic hearing ability pinpoints their origin and distance; its eyes focus, unblinking, pupils wide, on the spot. Something brown, largely concealed beneath a leaf, moves slowly. The Thinking Cat's computer whirrs silently and then it pounces with its front paws, claws completely extended, squarely on the back of a field mouse and delivers the killing bite. Having pawed briefly at the tiny corpse, the cat, which is not in a hungry mood, moves on to other diversions, its brief moment of sport over.

Nature's call

It is time to stop and defecate in one of the cat's favourite spots. It leaves the faeces uncovered for the enlightenment of the next cats to pass by; on its home territory, it would always carefully bury both the urine patches and faeces. Cats are more fastidious than dogs and do not like to soil on their own doorsteps.

The remains of the day

By late afternoon, the cat goes indoors for another long nap. When it awakes, it eats and enjoys playtime with its owner. Evening is perhaps its favourite time of day. Moths, frogs, hedgehogs, mice, bats and roosting birds are about – plenty of potential prey for the Thinking Cat to watch, if not to seriously hunt.

◀ **This cat's eyes are focused as it moves slowly and purposefully down the path. Alert and watchful, it is looking and listening all the time.**

◀ **Many owners leave food down for their cat to eat when it is ready and hungry. Often this is early in the morning before it goes out on a hunting foray in the garden.**

The cat's senses

More than any other kind of animal, the cat lives by its senses. A skilled hunter like its wild relatives (the tiger, leopard and cheetah), the domestic cat constantly collects information on its surroundings via highly-tuned sense systems. It interprets these messages and reacts appropriately – all cat behaviour is sense-based.

Vision

Perhaps the most important of all the cat's senses as it analyses information coming in from the world around it is its vision. The feline eye is constructed in much the same way as that of a human being, but there are important modifications that enable the animal to do certain things we cannot accomplish.

Night vision

Still basically a hunting animal, the domestic cat retains all the necessary perceptual abilities for the detection of prey that are used by the 'Tiger! Tiger! burning bright, in the forests of the night'. Many people believe that cats can see in the dark – not so. In a totally blacked-out room, a cat can see no better than you or me. What it can do, however, is gather the faintest quantities of light in its surroundings and enhance them. Even on a moonless night, the sky is never completely void of light; faint starlight or the pale reflections of high clouds are always present, and the cat's eye is specially designed to gather and use such minute scraps of luminosity.

It uses an ingenious method in the form of a 'mirror' (*tapetum lucidum*) placed behind the light-sensitive retina. This is composed of up to 15 layers of glittering cells. Faint light-beams enter the eye and pass through to hit and stimulate the light receptor cells of the retina. They then carry on past and are reflected by the 'mirror', so they contact the retina a second time. This 'double dose' multiplies the effect of the light and increases feline night vision immensely. We know that the domestic cat can make clear visual discrimination at one-sixth of the light levels required by humans.

The light receptor cells of the retina are of two types:
● Rods which are sensitive to low light levels
● Cones which provide resolving power.
With the cat retina containing more rods and fewer cones than a human's, cats see better than us in dim light but cannot discern fine detail quite as well as we can. The shining of the *tapetum lucidum* is what produces the characteristic golden or green gleam of a cat's eye in the dark.

Some bigger wild cats, such as pumas, have round pupils like humans, whereas the domestic cat has a vertical slit pupil. The virtue of a slit pupil is that it can close more efficiently and completely than a round one, thereby protecting the ultra-sensitive retina.

Field of vision

Another advantage for cats is that they have a wider angle of view than we possess. Our visual field is about 210 degrees of which 120 degrees are binocular. Cats have a visual field of 285 degrees, 130 degrees of which are binocular. The 130-degree binocular vision is another hunting adaptation that allows the animal to judge depth and distance with accuracy. In practice, there is more to judging distance than merely having binocular vision and cats are not quite as good as humans at estimating range. Humans make up for the somewhat narrower field by far more extensive eye movements, permitted by the larger area of white surrounding the cornea and iris.

▶ **A cat's eyes are very expressive and are a good indicator of its emotional state. Large pupils, such as the ones shown opposite, can indicate arousal or even excitement.**

Smell

The senses of smell and taste play a more important role for cats than for us. Inside the nose of mammals the lining membrane is folded in such a way that its surface area, containing specialized nerve endings that pick up molecules of chemicals in the air and then send signals via nerve fibres to the olfactory centre in the brain, is greatly enlarged. You and I get by with a mere five million of these nerve endings but a cat possesses around 19 million of them, and a long-nosed fox terrier an impressive 147 million.

Sensitivity

The cat's nose is particularly sensitive to odours containing nitrogen compounds. This ability enables the animal to detect, and reject, as every owner well knows, foods that are rancid or just slightly 'off', as these release chemicals rich in nitrogen.

But, in addition to smell, cats have a sense we lack. It is midway between smell and taste and has its own receptor, Jacobson's organ. This structure is linked to the roof of the mouth by a duct and transmits sensations to the brain's sexual centres. You can observe the Jacobson's organ in action when the cat indulges in the rather strange lip-curling, nose-wrinkling grimace known as 'flehming'. This behaviour brings the odours of some chemicals, particularly sexual ones, but also including those of catnip and valerian plants, in contact with the organ. Jacobson's organ is actually comparatively small and poorly developed in domestic cats and therefore 'flehming' is less obvious than in other regularly 'flehming' feline species, such as the lion or tiger.

▼ **Cats have a highly developed sense of smell and will investigate a wide range of objects to pick up clues about their environment and other animals passing through.**

The magic of catnip

Cats adore the highly scented plant catnip and will roll and sprawl ecstatically in this garden herb. Toms are more 'turned on' by catnip than queens. Why is this? The plant happens to contain an essential oil that is closely related to a substance excreted by a queen in her urine. A kitten's reaction to catnip is inherited. There seems to be a 'catnip gene', which 30 per cent of kittens do not have and, consequently, these individuals do not make a big fuss of the plant. Even those kittens that possess the gene will not usually respond to catnip's charms until they are about six months old. Catnip is also available in custom-made toys and cushions.

Scent marking

One important way of passing information between cats is by depositing scent signals through rubbing, scratching, urinating or the deliberate deposition of faeces (maddening). These chemical messages are put down in the environment for detection and decoding by another cat later on. A disadvantage of odour communication is that the signal cannot be altered easily and, once left, cannot be quickly removed. Consequently, cats have to be precise in their olfactory messaging and it is believed that most of the information carried by scent deposits is of a factual rather than an emotional nature.

Because of our poor sense of smell, we human beings cannot get involved in the cat's scent communication network. No doubt they do try to send us messages by scent marking, but we numbskulls unfailingly ignore or misinterpret them!

Taste

Cats are much fussier and 'faddier' eaters than dogs, which will more readily share a human diet, including sweet items. Like dogs and human beings, cats have taste buds in their mouth. They are situated in the small, backward-pointing protuberances (papillae) at the tip, sides and base of the tongue.

A temporary loss of the ability to taste, with accompanying loss of appetite, can occur in cats with respiratory disease, just as our taste buds are affected by a bad head cold. Some of our pet cats' wild relations find surprising things tasty. The Flat-headed cat (*Felis planiceps*) of the Far East, likes sweet potatoes, whereas tigers in Manchuria love to eat sweet nuts (shells and all), berries and fruit in the autumn.

A sweet tooth?

Whereas dogs have 'sweet' receptors in their taste buds, cats, as pure carnivores, do not. The mouth of the dog sends 'sweet' messages to the brain via sweet-sensitive nerve pathways. Until recently it was thought that no such sweet-sensitive pathways were to be found in the cat, but now scientists know that a few 'sweet'-bearing nerves do exist in the domestic cat and the numbers of them seem to be on the increase. Probably the breeding of cats that share the homes and habits (and titbits) of their human companions is stimulating, through the mechanism of natural selection, the use

Did you know?

Newborn kittens have a well-developed sense of taste but, in the same way as with us humans, this diminishes gradually with age.

and persistence of such structures. Certainly I have known a number of domestic cats, particularly Siamese and Burmese, that had a distinctly sweet tooth. Many cats, however, cannot digest sugar and develop diarrhoea if they consume much of it. Perhaps not having a sweet tooth is a natural aid to avoiding sugar.

◀ **Cats enjoy titbits and you can use them to reward good behaviour. it is best to use strongly smelling, tasty ones to get your cat interested.**

◀ **A healthy cat will enjoy his food. Loss of appetite can be a sign of a variety of health problems – both mild and serious – and you should consult your vet if this is the case.**

Hearing

The cat's sense of hearing is extremely acute. Cats and humans are about equal in their ability to locate the position of sounds, discriminating with around 75 per cent accuracy between two sounds that are separated by an angle of five degrees.

Accuracy and discrimination

Like us, the cat uses the elaborate shape of its outer ear to pick up variations in the quality of sound, and these variations help it to pinpoint the target. The skull of the cat contains two large echo chambers, which give it a high sensitivity to sounds on particular frequencies, such as high-pitched noises of the sort made by small prey animals. At high frequencies, a cat's hearing, like that of dogs, is far more acute than ours. A cat can hear sounds up to two octaves higher than the highest note we can hear, as well as sounds about half an octave higher than a dog can detect. In addition, the cat has great powers of discrimination between notes in the high frequency range; it can discriminate one-fifth to one-tenth of a tone difference between two notes.

As with us, a cat's sensitivity to high notes diminishes with age. This reduction in acuity can begin as early as three years of age, and is very marked by the time the cat is four-and-a-half years old.

▼ **The position of a cat's ears can give us vital clues to its emotional state. Ears facing forwards are a sign of an alert, confident cat or one who is happy and relaxed.**

Ear turning

Each external ear of a cat is worked by 30 muscles, as compared with merely six in man. This enables the animal to turn its ears with great precision in order to locate sounds. It is done far faster by a cat than by a dog.

Good balance

The ears of a cat are not just superbly equipped for hearing but they are also vital in facilitating the animal's amazing balancing ability. When a cat moves, and particularly if it falls, specialized structures within the inner ear, in conjunction with the eyes, transmit information to the brain on the position of the head in relation to the ground. As the head changes position or is subjected to changes in acceleration, crystals and liquid inside the inner ear are affected and their movement is detected by sensitive hairs. In just milli-seconds, the brain receives the signal and sends ultra-fast nerve commands to put it 'square with the ground. The rest of the body aligns with the head.

A newborn kitten has its inner ear mechanism fully developed, but because its eyes have not yet opened, it cannot see. Perfect balance requires a combination of eye and inner ear messages and, consequently, a kitten's righting reflex is not operational until the eyes open in the fullness of time.

◄ Most cats will enjoy rubbing against their owners' legs. This may be their way of greeting you or showing affection.

▲ Whiskers serve as a cat's sensitive antennae, locating and identifying objects that it cannot see when it is dark.

Touch

Cats love to touch. So often they greet their owners by giving them a gentle bump of their forehead or by rubbing against their legs, or they stroke the person's face with a paw when lying on their lap. The hairs of their coat are in contact with sensitive nerve receptors situated close to the hair roots.

The cat's whiskers

A specially developed area of a cat's touch involves its whiskers, although their function is not yet fully

understood. Removing the whiskers can distinctly disturb a cat for some time. A common belief is that they protrude on each side to a distance equal to the animal's maximum body width, rather like a measuring stick, thereby allowing it to judge whether or not it can pass through a given space without touching anything or perhaps making a give-away noise when stalking prey.

However, this is not true. Certainly, in darkness, the whiskers act as highly sensitive antennae. Their owner uses them to locate and identify things close by that it cannot see. In a similar way, sea lions hunting fish in deep, dark water, point their whiskers forwards as delicate probes. Should a cat's whisker touch a mouse in the dark, the cat reacts with the speed and lethal precision of a mousetrap.

Some scientists speculate that perhaps a cat bends some or all of its whiskers downwards when jumping or bounding over the ground at night – rather like the little desert jerboa which uses two of its whiskers to detect stones, holes or other irregularities in its path. Even when travelling at full speed, this little rodent can take avoiding action while in the air or on the ground by changing direction in a split second. Cats may well be able to do the same.

Did you know?

For a newborn kitten, the sense of touch is very important. Blind, with underdeveloped ears and no sense of smell as yet, touch is the vital sense that guides and reassures it when locating its mother's nipples at feeding time. The kitten responds to the vibrations produced by the queen purring and lying on her side. The vibrations say 'come and get it' and, sure enough, the mother stops purring as soon as the kitten begins to suckle.

Extra-sensory perception

Do cats possess other more mysterious senses that involve paranormal abilities? In the past, they have been associated with the supernatural and persecuted as familiars of the devil and witches, or even worshipped as demi-gods. Some people believe that cats have a sixth sense and are telepathic or psychic, although many of their so-called mysterious powers can be explained by the way they use the senses and abilities that science knows about. Here we examine the evidence.

Anticipating their owner's return

Many cats seem to know when their owner will arrive home from work. At the appropriate time, they perch on a windowsill or sit waiting behind the front door. Sure enough, they get it right, although, in many cases, their highly-tuned ears pick up the first, faint sound of the owner's familiar car engine approaching. Acute hearing does not explain all these incidents, however, particularly when the owner comes by taxi or walks from the bus stop. So far science has no rational explanation, so could it be extra-sensory perception?

Advance warning system

Cats may give advance warning of an impending earthquake or volcanic eruption. Strange behaviour by house cats was widely reported in the 10 to 15 minutes preceding the disasters of Agadir, Skopje and Alaska

in the 1960s. A German biologist present at the 1960 Chilean earthquake described cats becoming alarmed up to one minute before people were aware of the first tremors. Villagers on the slopes of Mount Etna in Sicily even keep cats as early warning devices. When the family cat drowsing by the fireside suddenly makes for the door at high speed, the human occupants know it is best to follow immediately. There is nothing supernatural about this feline behaviour – cats are just far more sensitive than their human owners to the first, faint vibrations underground.

In-built homing device

Cats can travel extremely long distances to find their home – but only in one direction. If a family takes their cat to a new home, their pet, seemingly preferring its old haunts and neighbourhood pals, can trek back. The longest journey on record for a cat returning home is held by a family pet in Oklahoma that was given to friends in California. Upon arrival, the cat, unimpressed by the glamour of the West Coast, set out to walk 1,400 miles back to its original owners. It took 14 months, but the cat was positively identified by X-rays confirming the presence of an old hip deformity.

Did you know?

Modern research suggests that the key to the homing ability of cats lies in a form of celestial navigation, rather like that used by birds. It is thought to work because, during the time that the cat lived in its original home, its eyes and brain automatically registered the angle of the sun at certain times of day.

Like many higher mammals, cats are thought to possess internal biological clocks. If they are uprooted to a new home where the sun's angle at a certain time of day is different from that to which they are accustomed, they want to put it right. They work by trial and error: moving in one direction, the angle gets worse but trying another, it improves, indicating the right direction to take.

The cat does not need a clear day – like birds, in overcast skies it uses polarized light from the sun. When, at last, the sun is in the right spot, the cat is in a neighbourhood with familiar sights, sounds and smells – nearly home.

Detecting mood changes

Volcanic eruptions and earthquakes are one thing, but can cats also detect mood changes in humans? How is it that they react appropriately to people who either love them or hate them? Many cat owners believe their cats can 'read' their moods. When I am cheerful and optimistic, my cats treat me differently from when I feel doubtful or preoccupied. Is it because they can detect changes in my voice or body language? We know that the chemical nature of our perspiration changes according to our mental state, but does a cat's acute sense of smell register this phenomenon or do they have some other way of weighing us up of which, as yet, we know nothing?

Telepathic powers?

How can one reasonably explain that when Shakespeare's friend, the Earl of Southampton, was imprisoned in the Tower of London, his black and white cat somehow discovered where he was being held, sought out the right cell, and entered by shinning down the chimney? A contemporary painting shows them in clink together. So might our cats also possess telepathic powers?

◀ **Many cats seem to sense when their owner is due home and will wait at a door or window, watching and listening for their footsteps or the sound of their car.**

How the cat has evolved

Over several millennia while the cat, as we now know it, was coming into being, the most important aspects of its nature – its senses – were gradually and crucially evolving. The necessary attributes of these quintessential hunter-killers were being refined by the genetic process of natural selection. The abilities of feline eyes, ears and noses, in particular, were being refined and enhanced. Progressively better senses inevitably led to better success in the hunt or the ambush.

Did you know?

When cats fall from a height, usually after being pushed or if the surface beneath them gives way, you might expect that the greater the height, the more injuries they would suffer. The fracture rate does increase steadily, the higher the storey from which poor Puss plummets but only up to a height of seven storeys. Higher than that, it begins to decrease!

When a cat falls through the air, its eyes and inner ear transmit information to the brain on the position of the head in relation to the ground. In fractions of a second, the brain sends nerve commands to the head to put it 'square' with the ground, the rest of the body aligns with the head and the cat reaches terra firma prepared for landing. After dropping for a distance of about five storeys, the cat reaches maximum speed. At this point, the speed is constant and the inner ear is no longer aware of, or stimulated by, any acceleration. So the cat relaxes and spreads its legs, like a freefall parachutist stabilizing his descent – relaxed bodies are less likely to fracture.

Tail: This is important in balance as well as feline communication.

Eyes: Important to a hunter, the cat's eyes are adapted for night vision. Involved in balance via the Righting Reflex (page 46).

Ears: Give powers of acute hearing, which are essential attributes for a hunter (page 48).

Whiskers: These give the cat a refined sense of touch in darkness (page 51).

Nose: For picking up scent 'messages', particularly when 'Flehming' takes place (page48).

Carpal pad: This is found above and behind the other pads on the forepaws. It is an anti-skidding device when landing from a jump.

Feline intelligence

There is no doubt that cats are highly intelligent – solitary, self-reliant hunters tend to be so. Their constructive use of their finely tuned senses is the core of their intelligence, and we have seen how cats can locate prey at night and find their way home over sometimes amazingly long distances. They can work out how to deal with problems, apply solutions and even adapt the solutions to different situations and circumstances.

How cats learn

Cats do learn. Many of their behaviour patterns are not instinctive but are copied from other cats. Kittens that are born to non-hunting mothers or lack littermates do not learn to hunt. Other habits, such as using a litter tray, may also be learned from the mother's example.

The first two-to-eight weeks of life are the critical learning period for cats. During this time they bond with their fellow felines and begin to interact with humans. Cats will carry their basic mistrust of people throughout their lives if they are not socialized and exposed to humans during this time, and this explains why feral cats are generally so misanthropic.

Inquisitive by nature, cats learn by observation followed by trial and error. Through careful study of human behaviour they can learn how to open doors, how waste paper baskets can be neatly flicked over and how an owner putting on an overcoat means that the front door will presently be opened, thereby

▼ Kittens learn their behaviours from their mother as well as from playing with littermates and being socialized to other felines, humans and other animals.

Did you know?

How can we measure the comparative intelligence of cats? Clearly, we cannot employ a written or oral IQ test. The yardstick most commonly used by biologists is to compare an animal's brain weight with the length of its spinal cord. This ratio shows how much grey matter controls how much body and thus it should be bigger in more intelligent species. The cat has a ratio of 4:1 as compared to a monkey's 18:1 and our 50:1.

stimulating a pet to go to the door in anticipation of a stroll outside. They use their learning ability and memory for useful 'operations', generally for their own gain, such as summoning humans by rattling objects, tapping on doors or launching themselves at a door knocker or bell, drinking water from a running tap or scooping milk from a jug with their paws.

Training a cat

Cats can be trained but not by coercion in the form of punishment. However, it is more difficult than training a dog – cats show none of the eagerness to please so commonly seen in dogs. Cat training requires much patience and a combination of rewards together with a system of communication, such as a clicker, which gives what animal trainers call a bridging signal. This signal acts as a link between the correct performance of a particular behaviour and the receiving of a reward in the cat's mind, although, ultimately, it will only cooperate if it is in the right mood to do so. Cats cannot be bought – that is part of their proudly independent character. Cats can and should be trained to use a litter tray and cat flap, or even to walk on a lead, sit up and beg and present a paw.

◄ You can also train your cat to do useful things, such as using a cat flap. Tempt it through the flap with a tasty treat.

Training guidelines

● Always reward good behaviour with praise and a tasty titbit – never use punishments.
● Train your cat before mealtimes, as food rewards are not so appealing to a pet with a full stomach.
● Keep the training sessions short to prevent boredom: 15 minutes is about right.
● Try to train your cat for 10-to-15 minutes every day.
● Be consistent with the training sessions to avoid confusion, always keeping the trainer, commands, signals and rewards exactly the same.

Intelligence

It is not easy to say which breed of cat is the most intelligent, and, as yet, there is no perfect yardstick for measuring feline IQ. In one study, a number of cat experts were surveyed for their opinions. The Siamese was consistently considered one of the brightest whilst the runners-up were the Bombay and the Egyptian Mau.

Intelligence test

To measure your cat's intelligence, try the following test. All you need is a hoop of approximately 60cm (24in) in diameter and a supply of your pet's favourite food treats. The objective is to see how quickly the cat learns to jump through the hoop. You will record the number of times you have to repeat the training command before the cat jumps through correctly.

1 Hold the hoop about 30cm (12in) above the floor with one hand and show the cat a treat held in the middle of the hoop with your other hand.

2 Give the training command, using a single word, such as 'Come' or 'Jump'.

3 Pull the treat back through the hoop. The cat must jump through to receive the reward.

When the cat has mastered this, you can stop holding the treat but position your hand in the same place. Reward the cat only if it jumps through the hoop. The test is completed when the cat jumps through the hoop on command at least two out of three times.

Scoring
The number of commands required in total for the jump to be mastered is fewer than 28 in the most intelligent cat; 40 to 48 in the average cat; and more than 60 in the below-average cat – but it's still a lovable, loyal pet, isn't it?

see also...

Scratching
page 84

Spraying
pages 82–83

Cat flap training
page 114

CHAPTER THREE

Talking cat

Domestic cats are highly social animals that communicate with one another and with their human friends in a variety of ways, including vocalization, body language, touch and scent production. Understanding how your cat 'communicates' with you and other cats will help you build a better, more rewarding relationship and will also make your pet more contented.

How cats communicate

Although cats are essentially lone hunters, they are not anti-social. Indeed, their intricate social interaction with their own kind includes different forms of communication: vocalization, body language, touch and scent. Feline 'conversations', with an exchange of information, attitudes and emotions, rely on a combination of sound, smell, sight and touch. We pet owners can, albeit imperfectly, join in some of these conversations and thereby strengthen our relationship with our cats.

Vocalization

A cat's repertoire of vocalizations ranges from plaintive mews and seductive purrs to incensed wails and irate screeches. Some pedigree breeds, such as the Siamese, are more vocal than others.

Body language

Feline body language consists of postures and tail positions that are enhanced by coat markings and facial expressions. The latter are emphasized by the markings that 'make up' the features.

Touch and scent

Cats also communicate by touch, rubbing noses and pressing their bodies against or grooming others. Using their highly sensitive noses, they identify other cats by their scents, sniffing one another's heads and beneath the tail, where odour-making glands are situated. Cats mark out their territory with scent 'markers', leaving messages for neighbouring felines (see page 64).

Cat communities

Even if your pet is the only feline in your household, if it is not confined as a house cat it will be part of a community of cats in your neighbourhood, street or apartment block. This community organizes itself into an 'association' with a built-in hierarchy, rituals and rules, which are laid down in a very precise way. All cats in the association know one another and are allotted positions in the hierarchy. Newly arrived strangers who are not in the club must fight to be accepted and allotted a place in the community.

▼ **Touch is important as a form of communicating. When cats rub against their owners they pick up and deposit scent as members of the same social group.**

▲ **This cat is vocalizing to let his owner know that he wants more food. Cats can make a variety of sounds that you will gradually learn to recognize.**

Hierarchies

Cat communities are matriarchies, the unneutered queen with the most kittens being at the top of the pecking order. When a queen is neutered, her social descent is very rapid. The male cats in a community form a hierarchy based on trials of strength. Rather like the Mafia, there is a pyramid of power based on 'respect' with a feline 'Godfather' at the top. The organization is rigid with occasional changes of position occurring when one member weakens and is overthrown in combat by an ambitious junior. Dominant toms do not possess large harems of queens and, in fact, are not necessarily given priority in the courtship stakes as of right. Curiously, queens sometimes select males well down the pyramid as mates. Top tom cats do, however, rule the biggest areas of territory, so it seems that land rather than sex is the key marker of social status in feline society.

Neutered toms have no place in the mafia 'family' – an entire tom with a social position gradually loses it after being castrated. After the operation the level of testosterone circulating in his blood steadily falls with the result that the masculine odour of his urine becomes weaker. As this happens, he gradually descends the social ladder, rung by rung, until he reaches the bottom.

It is little wonder that this busy social network of cats depends upon well-developed means of communication. Your pet makes itself felt and, hopefully, achieves its ends, both out of doors mingling with the neighbours' cats and indoors as part of your family, by the way it looks, acts, sounds – and smells.

▲ **All cats, from the oldest to the youngest, have a defined place in the feline hierarchy. Kittens learn the rules from an early age but may challenge their elders as they get older.**

Feline conclaves

A curious cat phenomenon that seems to involve a means of communication that we cannot detect is the so-called feline conclave. In cat society, meeting grounds are important centres of social intercourse. Males and females gather from time to time in these communal places, sitting peacefully in groups one to six metres from each other. Although the gatherings may sometimes involve the mating of a queen in season, most meetings are not sexual in nature. What goes on we simply don't know, but the assemblies certainly are not aimless. I like to think that there is some sort of communication – telepathy perhaps – between the club members and that these meetings are an important part of feline social life.

Body language

Cats can communicate with us and also with one another in a variety of different ways – by their body language and facial expressions as well as touch, vocalization and behaviour. By observing your cat closely, you can learn to recognize and read the signals. The body language, facial expressions and tail positions employed are additionally emphasised by the cat's coat markings.

The defensive cat

When faced with a display of aggressive behaviour from another animal, a cat's first reaction is to stand its ground.
- **Posture:** arched back, body turned sideways.
- **Ears:** flattened.
- **Pupils:** enlarged.
- **Whiskers:** bristling.
- **Tail:** bristling and arched.
- **Fur:** bristling along the back.
- **Mouth:** open, teeth on show. Emits hissing, spitting sounds.

The aggressive cat

A dominant cat uses its body language to encourage its opponent to turn tail and flee.
- **Posture:** poised to strike.
- **Ears:** pricked, furled back.
- **Pupils:** closed to a slit.
- **Whiskers:** bristling forwards.
- **Tail:** low and close, bristling and swishing to and fro.
- **Fur:** smooth.
- **Mouth:** wide open with lips curled back to enhance the snarl. Makes growling, hissing and spitting sounds.

▼ **The defensive cat looks ferocious with its bristling whiskers, mouth wide open, and enlarged pupils, hissing and spitting furiously at its feline opponent.**

▲ **The pupils of an aggressive cat narrow to a slit as it opens its mouth wide and bares its teeth, ears pricked and whiskers bristling as it prepares to strike.**

▲ This cringing cat is exhibiting typical submissive body language, with its tail held low and ears back.

The submissive cat

Faced with an aggressor for which it is no match, the submissive cat communicates its submission by its body language.
- **Posture:** cringing.
- **Ears:** flattened.
- **Pupils:** enlarged.
- **Whiskers:** flattened.
- **Tail:** thumping the ground.
- **Fur:** flattened.
- **Mouth:** may open but not emit any sound, or half open with the emission of a distress call.

The importuning cat

Another form of body language is employed by the importuning cat, which is intent on obtaining a favour from a human being, such as a morsel of food or asking for a door to be opened.
- **Posture:** raised head.
- **Ears:** pricked.
- **Eyes:** wide open, alert and gazing intently at the object of the cat's desire.
- **Tail:** held up, often moving languidly.
- **Mouth:** emits a range of noises, some of which have been identified as specifically begging for attention or, particularly, for food, and which are directed at the cat's owner.

The contented, relaxed cat

The signs of a happy cat are easy to recognize.
- **Eyes:** eloquently convey the telltale signs of a contented, happy cat – watch out for slow blinking.
- **Ears:** a confident, alert and happy animal's ears will face forwards or may tilt back slightly.
- **Tail:** slow, graceful and sweeping.
- **Fur:** smooth but not tightly flattened to the back.
- **Mouth:** may purr but not necessarily.

▲ **This tabby is adopting an importuning posture, with head raised and ears pricked, as it gazes up at is owner, asking for food.**

▲ **When cats approach each other, their body language will change and adapt to the circumstances. Their tail position, posture and ears provide us with valuable clues.**

Olfactory communication

A cat's sense of smell is more highly developed and more able to discriminate than ours. Although its head is smaller than a human's, a cat carries around 19,000,000 specialized nerve endings in its nose for detecting smells. We get by with a mere 5,000,000. Cats also possess a sense we lack, which is midway between taste and smell and has its own receptor, the Jacobson's organ. You can see a cat using this when it makes the curious lip-curling, nose-wrinkling grimace known as Flehming.

Scent glands

Your pet's equivalent of exchanging names and handshakes involves sniffing the other cat's head or beneath its tail. These are the places where scent glands are concentrated and the aromas they produce, undetectable by you and me, convey a wealth of personal information. Other glands in the cat's skin also produce scent. When he or she rubs against you or other animals, the scent left both identifies the individual they have marked and also indicates their status in feline society to another cat.

▼ **Cats like to roll and mark the ground with their unique scent. This leaves a signal for other animals that pass by. They also use scratch marks, urine and faeces.**

Spraying

Other smell signals are carried in a cat's urine and faeces. Your pet urinates deliberately when marking its territory, and the spraying routine follows an unchanging pattern. The area sprayed and the number of squirts never vary. Spraying is normally, but not exclusively, done from a standing position, so the urine is deposited at nose height, perfectly placed to be detected by any passing cat. Cats of both sexes, neutered and un-neutered, spray mark.

Did you know?

When a cat scratches a tree it is not done principally, as is commonly supposed, just to keep its claws in good condition. The visible scratch marks, together with the scent deposited by the feet, send messages to other cats regarding ownership of territory. They serve as visual markers and scent signposts.

Sebaceous glands

Sebaceous glands in a cat's skin produce the oil necessary to keep the coat in good condition. These glands are modified in certain areas, such as the chin and root of the tail, to secrete chemicals that provide useful information. The cat's highly sensitive nostrils can detect subtle changes in these chemicals.

When a cat passes motions as part of its regular bowel function, it will always try to bury the droppings by scratching with its hind feet. When, however, the droppings are laid down as territory markers, no attempt is made to cover them up. So often, to your embarrassment, these calling cards are placed prominently on the tops of fences or, even worse, on your next-door neighbour's lawn.

Territory marking.

Cats mark their territories and objects they consider to be theirs, including people's legs on occasion, by urine spraying, scratching and rubbing. Each cat's urine has a scent that is unique to it alone. Other cats coming across a patch of sprayed urine can identify the individual that left it. The human nose, however, cannot distinguish between the urine of different cats, not that we would want to!

Scratching leaves a visible mark and deposits scent from the animal's feet, whereas rubbing against a solid object is yet another way of staking a claim to something, leaving scent from the sebaceous glands in the cat's skin (see box above).

▶ **Cats encountering a new scent will spend some time sniffing it and trying to interpret its message. In order to do this, they rely on their Jacobson's organ.**

Playing with your cat

Playing games with your cat is an effective way of communicating with each other. Play is not just for pleasure; it is important for a cat's wellbeing. It aids bonding, gives your pet a valuable opportunity to practise survival skills, provides exercise and is an important part of the learning process. Through play, a kitten learns about the physical laws governing the world: how fast it needs to run after, and at what angle to intercept, moving prey; and how much of a thrust of the hind legs it needs to jump and land on an object some distance away. By means of play, you can progress to training your pet.

The name game

The contented cat and, indeed, the contented owner can develop a good relationship with one another. The first and easiest step is the name game. It is very important that your cat is trained to know and respond to its name as soon as possible after arriving in your household. Take some time out to teach it.

Whether you choose a long or a short name, it must be one that you can call out clearly and easily. Single-syllable words are obviously the easiest to use, but two or even three syllables seem to work just as well.

Use your cat's name frequently, particularly at feeding and treat-giving times as well as at every regular grooming, bonding and play session.

Action games

● All cats love cardboard boxes – they jump in and out of them, often ambushing passers-by. Provide one for your pet – nothing could be simpler or cheaper.
● If your cat has outdoor access, tree-climbing provides abundant exercise. A climbing frame should be installed for a housebound cat.
● Cats enjoy chasing ping-pong balls or rolled-up balls of tin foil around obstacles like chairs.
● Fishing-rod toys, which comprise a stick and a length of elastic or string with a toy on the end, are excellent for interactive play. But beware: never leave a cat alone with such a toy as the elastic or the string may get wrapped round its neck.
Note: All games are more beneficial if you have two cats as they will compete for a toy.

Did you know?

Play is a notable feline activity and wild cats play with as much eager enthusiasm as their domestic relatives. Because play is generally most pronounced in animal species where the young pass through a relatively prolonged period of 'childhood', carnivores, including cats, are among the most playful of mammals and, naturally, their young play more than adults. Even a simple tin foil ball can keep a kitten amused.

Kittens love to play and explore. It is all part of learning about their environment. Brightly coloured toys that move are always very popular.

see also...

Aggression
pages 76–79

Games
pages 108–109

Spraying
pages 82–83

CHAPTER FOUR

Common problems

Cats sometimes develop bad habits, which can be problematic for owners, especially if they are taking on an adult rescue cat that has long been set in its ways. Let's look at the possible causes of such behaviour, how it can be prevented and the positive action you can take to resolve it.

Behaviour problems

The happy, contented cat does not usually develop any bad habits in or around the house, but, as ever, prevention is always better than cure and it is up to you, the owner, to try to identify likely causes and then take positive action to eliminate them.

Possible causes

The most common instigators of unwelcome behaviour in cats are psychological: anxiety, stress, loneliness, boredom, grief at the loss of a human or feline companion, problems with other cats in the house or neighbourhood, especially concerning territory, and, in some cases, poor health.

A variety of infections, toxins, tumours, traumatic damage and hormonal disturbances can cause pronounced changes in a cat's behaviour, and we now know that a condition known as Feline Spongiform Encephalopathy, the cat version of 'Mad Cow Disease' and variant Creuztfeldt-Jacob Disease of humans, sometimes occurs in cats and affects their actions.

Spraying

The spraying of urine by cats is not always associated with territory marking or sex. Occasionally a cat will spray on the legs of a family member. This is what I call the 'I love you' sort of spraying and it is the cat's rather embarrassing way of indicating ownership.

▼ Every owner wants a contented cat that will curl up happily and snooze in the sunshine. This is achievable if you keep your pet happy and prevent future problems.

◀ Rewarding desirable behaviour with a tasty treat will help reinforce good habits and prevent many common behaviour problems developing.

▶ **Behaviour problems can sometimes arise in elderly cats. They may become nervous, grumpy and withdrawn or forget to use the cat flap and have toileting accidents inside the house.**

Did you know?

The kind of feline behaviour which I call 'sense of humour' spraying I have only seen in lions. A good example of this was the old male lion at Manchester Zoo who would wait until a crowd of admiring visitors gathered close to the weld-mesh fence of his enclosure and then slowly turn so that his rump was towards them. Suddenly, without warning, he would eject a stream of urine with great accuracy through the mesh and onto the face of someone in the front row. How the big cat's audience roared with laughter! The hapless victim, reeking of entire lion urine, would stagger back out of the crowd as another of the still-chortling onlookers moved into his vacated space. Little did they know that the lion had another load waiting, which he would presently jet with perfect aim at his next victim.

Age can also be a factor in causing problem behaviour, particularly in cases of soiling around the house. Elderly cats may simply become forgetful and careless in their personal habits. A specific syndrome known as Feline Cognitive Dysfunction, in which areas of degeneration appear in the brain, similar to those of Alzheimer's Disease in man, can affect older cats and lead to alterations in social interaction, loss of house training and a diminished ability to learn and remember.

Bad behaviour can also be seasonal; for example, it is more likely to occur in cold, wet winter months when cats are often more housebound and boredom sets in. Cats are creatures of habit and they often do not respond well to change. Thus, a new individual, animal or human coming into the family home can sometimes trigger changes in a resident cat's behaviour.

If you decide to take on an adult cat from a rescue organization, do be aware that your new pet may arrive with its own emotional and behavioural problems and it may take time to settle in. If it displays problem behaviours, try to discover the causes or triggers and work patiently to resolve the problem.

Correcting problem behaviour

You will need plenty of patience when you embark on the task of correcting your pet's behaviour. In all cases, it is essential that you give your cat plenty of love, attention and good living conditions – a safe, snug bed and enough food and water. Talk regularly to your cat, using its name and in a warm, friendly tone of voice. Always remember that cats do not respond to force, either in the short or long term. Punishment of any kind must never be used and would probably be counter-productive, reinforcing the animal's feelings of stress and anxiety. Corrective training is by reward, usually in the form of food treats.

Identifying possible triggers

Try to identify any factors or changes in the world around your cat that might be triggering the unwelcome behaviour and then, if possible, take appropriate steps to improve things. Don't delay – the longer the behaviour exists, the more difficult to eradicate it may become. If you continue to have problems with your pet after reading this chapter, you may consider contacting an animal behaviour expert – many specialize in cats. Ask your vet to recommend a suitable behaviourist and get in touch with them.

◀ Housebound cats may spend hours looking wistfully out of windows at a more exciting world outside. They need toys, mental stimulation and games to keep them occupied and busy.

◀ Some cats are loners by nature but others enjoy human company and like 'helping' their owners in the garden. However, take care that they do not scratch up your treasured plants.

The nervous cat

A cat's fears can be generated by objects, other living things or by events. It is easy to understand how the vacuum cleaner or the appearance of the cat basket might frighten a pet but some cats react in alarm irrationally. One of my Birmans is inordinately scared of kitchen foil. He has never been hurt by foil, but the metallic sound of it being handled sends him scurrying.

Travelling containers

Cats can be afraid of a variety of things, including some common and seemingly innocuous items. A relatively common one is the travelling case. To the cat, this little mobile prison can be a threat, an unwelcome reminder of visits to the vet or boarding kennels. Therefore you should select a travelling case with the utmost care. A roomy, comfortably-lined container will please a cat better than a small cardboard box.

Always allow your cat to familiarize itself with whatever container you obtain before placing your pet inside it. Leave it somewhere in the house where the cat can explore and get used to it and perhaps even use it as regular sleeping accommodation. Giving the animal a favourite treat when it is settled in the container will enhance its appeal. This approach should be adopted where other objects are a source of fear to your pet.

▲ If your cat is nervous of going in its cat carrier, put a tasty treat inside to tempt it in and allow it to explore.

▼ If your cat is fearful and anxious, you need to encourage interaction with its environment to give it more control.

Hidden behaviours

Some cats are frightened by a particular thing or someone they encounter. The trigger may be a sudden noise, the sound of the vacuum cleaner or the arrival of a visitor, and off the cat shoots to hide under the sideboard. Such a cat may be agoraphobic, detesting open spaces and resenting changes in its surroundings. Life is full of anxiety and may worsen to the point where it is in hiding for most of the day. Rescued cats are somewhat more likely to behave in this way.

The causes of this distressing behaviour are likely to lie in the cat's early life and poor socialization. For example, it may not have been in contact with, or been handled by, human beings in its important first two months of kittenhood, or it may have received poor parenting from its mother.

How to cope with a fearful feline

The younger the cat is, the greater the chance of success. However, whatever its age, you will need abundant patience. Begin by instigating regular sessions of familiarization and friendship where only you and the cat are together. Play some simple games, stroke the cat frequently and keep talking to it gently. Have plenty of treats to hand. Eventually, as the cat becomes less fearful, other people and objects can be introduced into the sessions. If your pet is xenophobic, start by bringing in other members of the family before progressing gradually to introducing strangers.

Agoraphobia

True agoraphobia is fear of open spaces outside the home. The cause is nearly always some form of unpleasant past experience: a neighbour's bellicose tom, perhaps, or a loudly barking dog. In severe cases, the cat may prefer to revert to a permanent indoor life. Thousands do so happily, provided that they have a litter tray, toys and a snug bed.

If your cat likes to go outside but is deterred by the possibility of bumping into whatever it is that disturbs it, erect an enclosed mesh pen (the type breeders use for queens with litters) in your garden. Put the cat inside the pen each day; initially, for only a short time, but gradually extend its length of stay. Feed and play with your pet in the pen, so it grows fond of its surroundings. Eventually, under your supervision, the cat will go into the garden without being put in the pen, although it should remain in place.

▲ Spend time with your cat, stroking it, playing games and offering favourite treats to help it relax and be less fearful. Socialise the cat to a range of noises, objects and people.

Cat flaps

If you haven't already got one, installing a cat flap is a wise precaution for a fearful cat. If a scary experience does occur outside, your cat can escape back into the safety of its home.

The aggressive cat

There are several forms of feline aggression, but the four main ones are male-on-male aggression, fear-provoked aggression, territorial aggression and competitive aggression. Cats can learn to be aggressive as, for example, when the animal uses a nip of the teeth or a quick flash of a paw to gain a desired result. Re-directed aggression occurs when the cat vents its displeasure on someone or something other than the actual cause of whatever it was that upset Puss in the first place.

Male-on-male aggression

This is the classic cat fight, which is usually caused by the presence of a female in heat nearby, and the combat is part of a tom's struggle to maintain its status within the neighbourhood cat hierarchy.

● Treatment of the condition is by castration, although aggression can still flare up occasionally between two neutered male cats. Progestagen contraceptive preparations can control serious fighting between neutered toms in a multi-cat household. If you are experiencing these problems, ask your vet for advice.

Fear-provoked aggression

This is defensive fighting by a fearful scaredy cat forced to face up to something that frightens it, perhaps by being put outside into a garden that holds unnamed terrors. Defensive cat fighting differs in style from the male-on-male variety with little or no use of the teeth, at least at first. Neutering does not affect fear aggression, although some vets suspect too much proprietary canned or pelleted food in the diet may be a contributory factor.

● Treatment is usually of the kind previously described for the nervous cat (see pages 74–75).

Diet

Fear aggression can be inherited from nervous parents, in which case upbringing and learning are both very important. Some veterinary experts suspect that diet may play a part in feline aggression. Certain additives in proprietary cat foods may have an effect in stimulating aggressiveness. Giving fresh food, cooked chicken, boiled fish, boiled rice and the like instead of canned, foil-packaged or pelleted cat foods could calm down certain individual animals.

Territorial/competitive aggression

Territorial and competitive aggression are similar insofar as conflict arises when a cat considers that its 'rights and privileges' are being challenged. Castration may help, but the problem tends to fade away in a multi-pet household with the passage of time as the cats organize their in-house relationships.

● Owners must handle the introduction of new members into their family home with care and patience. New babies can often put a resident cat's nose out of joint, and you should prepare for the new arrival by accustoming your pet to the sights, sounds and smells of all the nursery paraphernalia as soon as possible. When the baby arrives, pay extra attention to the cat in the presence of the infant.

▲ **Always take care when introducing a new cat to young children. Supervise them carefully at all times and never leave them alone together. Children can get very excitable and frighten a cat, causing it to scratch or bite.**

Did you know?

Some cats will try to get away unscathed from an aggressive opponent by doing nothing more than simply crouching, not moving a muscle and, crucially, avoiding eye contact. It is almost as if they are hoping to become invisible. At the first opportunity, often when the aggressor pauses or is distracted, the cat then slips away.

Re-directed aggression

A cat can re-direct aggression and vent its displeasure on someone or something other than whatever has upset it. This unwarranted retribution may be delivered immediately or even at some later date. For example, a cat that has returned from the vet may think: 'You took me to that awful guy and he stuck a needle into me! Someone's gonna feel sorry!' Whereupon it sharply nips the hand of some family member, not necessarily the person involved in the visit to the surgery. The mood of such a cat has elements of fright and agitation within it.

● Tranquillizers, such as Valium, can sometimes be valuable in treating this condition. Unfortunately, however, some cats that re-direct in this manner do not respond to medication and can only be treated by love and attention from their owners.

Excessive grooming

A curious form of feline aggression is when your cat who is, apparently, thoroughly enjoying lying on your lap being stroked, suddenly bites your hand or arm,

The cat's purr

Where does the cat's purr come from? Many scientists believe it is produced by a large vein in the chest cavity. Where the vein passes through the diaphragm, muscles contract around the vein – when the back is arched, for example – 'nipping' the blood flow and setting up oscillations, whose sound is magnified by the air-filled bronchial tubes and windpipe, However, very recent research suggests that the sound originates, as originally supposed, in the larynx or 'voice-box'.

jumps off and walks, always unhurriedly, away. Cats don't groom one another for lengthy periods and sometimes too much grooming by you, their owner, seems to irritate them to the point of warning you off. The answer to this problem, as you might expect, is not to over-groom or make too much fuss of your pet.

▶ **Some cats do not like being held by their owners and may try to escape when they are picked up. Do not over-fuss your cat if it does not enjoy the attention.**

◀ Some cats, especially Siamese, enjoy human company and love to be fussed over and stroked. They are often gentle with children and like to join in family activities.

Soiling 'accidents' indoors

Undoubtedly, the behavioural problem that most cat owners complain about is urinating or defecating in a totally inappropriate place inside the house, such as on a bed or a carpet. Suddenly, it seems, the cat loses all its litter training – but why?

Causes of indoor toileting

If your cat starts to have 'accidents' inside the house, instead of punishing it, you should try to discover the reasons for the problem behaviour. There may be an underlying health problem that needs checking out by the vet or it could simply be old age.

Health problems
Indoor urination or defecation can sometimes indicate the existence of some underlying medical problem. Kidney disease, diabetes (common in cats) and cystitis (bladder inflammation) could be involved. Irritation caused by crunchy 'gravel' in the bladder of a cat that does not or cannot drink enough water can make urination painful for the animal. As a result, it passes water irregularly, often painfully, wherever it can and frequently in the wrong place. A normal cat will associate urination with its litter tray, so when urination becomes painful, it may link the tray to an unpleasant experience and thus decline to use it.

Similarly, defecation out of the litter tray may be due to a bowel upset, particularly diarrhoea. In such cases, the cat may not have time to reach the tray before the 'accident' happens, so owners should inspect their pet's stools. They can come in a range of colours and be caused by infectious, parasitic or digestive factors. If the diarrhoea lasts more than 48 hours, consult your vet.

Elderly cats
Senior citizen cats can, of course, develop 'accidental' tendencies when they are very old. The sphincter muscles of the urinary tract and anus can weaken and become rather too relaxed. You cannot do much about such geriatric behaviour except forgive your old friend, clean up the mess and forget about it.

Did you know?

You can use both cat pheromone sprays and vaporizers to control spraying (see page 82). These sprays, such as Feliway, can be applied directly to the surfaces on which a cat sprays. In a recent study, it was found that application of the chemical twice daily for one month stopped marking completely in 33 per cent of households and reduced it markedly in a further 57 per cent of homes, so if you are experiencing this problem with your pet it is worth investing in these products.

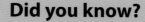

◀ **Elderly cats may be prone to 'accidents' around the house as they get older and lose control of their bladder.**

Litter tray checklist

In younger cats, the psychological causes of litter-tray training breaking down are many and various. Consider the following possibilities and then act positively to resolve the problem.

● Is the litter tray 'putting the cat off' in some way?

● Has the litter material been changed? Some mineral-based material may be more unpleasant to tread on, and some animals hate the chlorophyll odour-eating compounds added to certain types of litter.

● Has the cat recently been alarmed in some way when using its tray?

● Is the litter changed and the tray cleaned often enough?

● Has any strong-smelling disinfectant been used in cleaning the litter tray? Simply scrubbing it with some washing-up liquid is sufficient.

● In a multi-cat household, has a more submissive individual been harassed or denied access to the litter tray by another resident cat?

● Are there enough litter trays for each cat, ideally with one extra tray?

● Has the litter tray been moved to a place that is less congenial to peaceful voiding?

● Is the cat getting too plump and portly to pass with ease through the doorway of a covered tray?

● Is an old cat, perhaps troubled with arthritis, having to go upstairs to a litter tray on another floor? Or are the sides of the tray too high for it to step over comfortably?

● Was the cat inadvertently shut in or in some way denied access to the litter tray?

● Could the cat have been stressed by, say, moving house, the rearrangement of furniture, the arrival of new household members or workmen?

The spraying cat

You must never confuse the deliberate spraying of urine by a cat with the accidental toilet-training breakdowns discussed on pages 80–81. Spraying is not only carried out by uncastrated toms but also by neutered toms and, occasionally, by females.

Leaving a message

Spraying is essentially the cat's way of marking territory or property by leaving an olfactory message for other felines. The cat backs up to some vertical surface, raises its tail, makes its rear end quiver, makes treading movements with its back feet and then ejects a small squirt of urine backwards. The performance may be repeated two or three times.

This behaviour is mainly a sign of anxiety in a cat that feels its personal living space or its own possessions are under threat, perhaps in a multi-cat household where there is significant competition between males. It may also occur if an outside cat, particularly an entire tom, enters the house through the cat flap in search of food or leaves a malodorous calling-card on the doorstep. The presence of a queen in oestrus nearby can also trigger the behaviour.

Occasionally, a cat will cause a degree of consternation in the family by spraying on the legs of a person. Do not misinterpret this – it is not a manifestation of anxiety but rather a quasi-proprietorial one. The cat is saying in its own rather unique way: 'I love you!'

Did you know?

The newest aids in tackling this type of aberrant behaviour are sprays and electric vaporizers containing a form of cat skin gland pheromone. The pheromone is picked up by the delicate feline nostril and passes to the brain via the blood stream. The effect in most, but not all, cats is to stop urine marking and to make the animals calmer and more settled.

Resolving the problem

You must try to identify the trigger factors for your cat's spraying in order to eliminate them. Here are some basic guidelines to help you resolve the problem.

Cleaning

Always thoroughly clean any sprayed areas with a proprietary deodorizing liquid and then, hopefully, render them undesirable to your pet by using a deterrent spray or putting down mothballs.

▶ **If your cat sprays indoors, it is important to clean up thoroughly with disinfectant to remove all traces of the smell and to prevent further incidences occurring.**

◀ Cat flaps give cats the freedom to come and go as they please. However, they can also be used by strange cats, so you may have to protect them.

Cat flaps

If a feline usurper is coming in via the cat flap, install one that will open only when your cat, carrying a small magnetic gadget on its collar, is in close proximity to it.

Toilet training

An increasing number of cat owners, particularly in the United States, are training their cat to use the family lavatory, so obviating the need for a litter tray. The training takes two to three months, with an aluminium foil cooking tray taking the place of the litter tray and fixed over the toilet bowl. A hole, which is gradually increased in size, is made in the tray and, if all goes well, the cat ends up using the toilet like a sitting human being.

Neutering

Neutering all the cats in the household will often help to control or solve a spraying problem, but neutered animals sometimes spray, too, although the urine of neutered toms is much less pungent than that of entire toms. If in doubt, ask your vet for advice.

Play zones

Where feasible, you might be able to convert spraying areas into feeding or playing zones, thereby deterring the cat from soiling them. The litter tray could be placed in the spraying area and then gradually moved an inch or two each day nearer to its proper place.

Veterinary help

In some cases of indoor spraying, medication by your vet with the use of tranquillizer or contraceptive preparations can prove effective, but these treatments are usually a last resort. If you really cannot solve the problem yourself, ask your vet for advice.

The scratching cat

Cats scratch for a variety of reasons – to leave visual territorial markers for other cats, to keep their claws in good shape by removing the old, outer layers, to exercise the muscles and tendons of their forelegs, and also, it would seem, because they like the 'feel' and the texture of the surface beneath their feet.

Natural behaviour

Scratching is a natural behaviour that, ideally, would only be performed outside the house. Unfortunately, some cats often start doing it indoors. Favourite scratching places include the backs of sofas and armchairs and embossed wallpaper. Where a cat scratches in several different places inside the house, there may be psychological causes, such as insecurity and stress involving territorial rights, induced, for example, by the arrival of a new cat in the household or the visits of outsider toms who come spraying on doorsteps or window-sills.

Prevention and cure

How can you stop this type of destructive behaviour? Custom-made scratching posts and pyramids or blocks of compressed corrugated paper (all widely available from pet stores) will help resolve the problem.

A do-it-yourself version of a scratching post can be made at home by wrapping a log in some coarse sacking and, best of all, impregnating it with some catnip extract. Strategically place the posts in places where your cat may feel vulnerable, such as beside doors or exits to the outside world.

Watch your cat carefully and as soon as you see it contemplating a scratching bout on a valued piece of furniture or wallpaper, grab your pet and take it immediately to the acceptable scratching location.

When your cat scratches in the correct place, give it lavish vocal praise and a tasty food treat as a reward for good behaviour. Begin training young cats as early as possible in this way, so they make the right associations and you protect your furniture and home.

▶ **A scratching post must be high enough for the cat to scratch at full stretch to adequately exercise his claws.**

The gardening cat

Some cats delight in gardening – in your garden. One thing they particularly like doing is digging up the bulbs you have just planted and then watching you plant them all again.

Preventing digging

To counter such horticultural felines, try strategically placing some pieces of lemon peel or cat repellent granules around the bulbs or you could try spraying them with a cat repellent aerosol. Another good deterrent is to place some wire mesh on the ground covering the bulbs. The plants will grow through the mesh but the cat will hate walking on it. If you are in the garden when the cat starts digging, a quick squirt from a water bottle or turning on a lawn sprinkler can be used as an effective sign of your disapproval.

Eating houseplants

Many cats will enjoy the occasional nibble at plants, including houseplants. This habit is very difficult to stop and, unless the plants are poisonous (see page 33), is of little consequence. Prevention being better than cure, you should avoid having any poisonous species either indoors or outside in the garden.

Indoor cats

The best way to prevent an indoor cat from nibbling houseplants is to provide some trays of seedling grass sprouts. Most cats find these more attractive and will consume them happily, even if they have access to a garden and some outdoor grass and plants. The trays are available from most good pet stores and usually prove an excellent investment.

▼ **Many cats are interested in houseplants and develop an inappropriate appetite for this plant material.**

The over-grooming cat

Cats are fastidious creatures that take great pride in their appearance. The normal cat spends 30 to 40 per cent of its waking hours grooming itself – combing and licking its fur with its rather abrasive tongue. Over-grooming is a psychological condition, which can sometime go so far that fur is lost and bald patches appear.

Obsessive-compulsive disorder

Over-grooming is, in reality, a stereotypic or obsessive-compulsive abnormity of behaviour in the same class as the incessant pacing to and fro of zoo tigers or polar bears. However, before deciding that a particular cat is an over-groomer, it is important to examine it to eliminate the possibility that an itchy skin, perhaps as a result of an allergy to flea bite saliva, or some other kind of irritating dermatitis, might lie at the root of the phenomenon. Ask your vet if you are unsure.

A true obsessive-compulsive disorder, such as over-grooming, is an abnormal, excessive, unnecessary, recurring behaviour over which the cat has absolutely no control. It cannot decide when to start or to stop it but is simply driven to do it.

Causes and motivation

The initial causes can be boredom or stress if the cat is anxious about or in conflict with some aspect of its environment or lifestyle. Some cases are not induced by such external circumstances or events but are internal, triggered by chemical or electrical changes in the brain. An owner can unwittingly reinforce the abnormal behaviour by giving treats or paying special attention to their pet, both of which are interpreted by the cat as rewards. Eventually, however, the bizarre behaviour becomes ingrained and continues even if the original source of motivation no longer exists.

Treatment

How can you treat such a cat? Firstly, it is important to try to identify the original cause of the compulsion. There may be a variety of reasons to you to consider.

▼ **When grooming is a calming technique and used as a displacement activity it can become excessive. Stress, such as fear and anxiety, can cause over-grooming.**

All cats will scratch themselves from time to time and this is a natural behaviour as is a normal degree of self-grooming to keep the coat in good condition. Relaxed cats do not over-groom.

Ask yourself the following questions:
- Is there a new member in your household?
- Is an outside cat trying to usurp your pet's territory and acting belligerently?
- Has the cat's favourite sleeping spot been disturbed?
- In a multi-cat household, are the social relationships between the various animals rather fragile?

Mild over-grooming need not be treated if there are no physical ill effects in the cat. If treatment is deemed necessary, try distracting the cat by making a sudden sharp noise – a short blast from a whistle, clapping your hands, striking a gong – or squirting it briefly with a water pistol. As soon as it is distracted, promote alternative behaviour by lavishing your attention on your pet and starting a game or proffering a toy.

Above all, it is essential that the cat gets plenty of attention – day by day – and is regularly handled and played with. You should provide a snug, peaceful place where the cat can rest and a variety of interesting toys and other objects to prevent boredom setting in.

If all else fails, your vet may prescribe some medication, such as Prozac, and, particularly in the United States, clomipramine. However, this is a last resort.

Stress and anxiety

The commonest cause of odd feline compulsive behaviour, where physical ailments are not involved, is stress or anxiety of some kind. If you can't pinpoint what it is inside your home that may be causing the problem, you should investigate outside. Has a new dog arrived next door? Has a swaggering, un-neutered tom taken to visiting your garden on a regular basis?

Other obsessive-compulsions

There are a number of other rather peculiar behaviour patterns that cats can exhibit. Although some of them may be amusing for you to watch and not prejudicial to the cat's wellbeing, others, such as those involving bizarre appetites, can lead to serious medical problems and, as a responsible owner, you should deal with them.

Fabric chewing

This is more commonly found in Oriental breeds, particularly Burmese and Siamese. The behaviour typically starts at between two and eight months of age. Many pets begin with wool and then move on to other fabrics. Balls of wool are especially dangerous, as the rasp-like upper surface of the tongue tends to push the wool towards the back of the mouth where it is often swallowed. Once swallowing starts, it tends to continue with the result that the stomach and intestines become full of wool. I have seen one Burmese with brown wool trailing out of its mouth and also its anus. That patient had to have an immediate operation in which its abdomen was opened and then incisions made at a number of places in the bowel wall to extract the wool in pieces. To pull one end of the protruding wool would have caused fatal damage by making the intestines 'concertina' with the material cutting into the delicate gut lining at several points.

'Twitchy cat disease'

This is where the animal's skin suddenly ripples and twitches. The cat may jump up and run to nowhere in particular and for no obvious reason, sometimes seemingly hallucinating. It is frightened but does not know why. This phenomenon is probably a transient upset in the neuro-chemistry of the brain.

Did you know?

The slow process of the ageing of their brain cells can lead to behavioural changes in old cats. Although these changes are not usually troubling, some pets become more nervous and withdrawn. They realize that their powers are fading and their ability to cope, particularly in feline social relationships, is weakening.

Other behaviours

Some behaviours can be obsessive-compulsive but not always; they include the cat biting at its flanks, legs or tail, urine-spraying in undesirable places, tail-chasing, repetitive bouts of vocalization, chewing or plucking out its own fur, and bizarre appetites. With the latter, the cat may take to eating things such as candle wax, plastic, paper or coconut matting.

Causes and treatment

The causes of all these various forms of obsessive-compulsive behaviour are generally the same as those described for over-grooming, the principal ones being some form of stress or anxiety. The owner or vet will use the same methods in tackling the problem (see page 87). With bizarre appetites, it is important to ensure by means of veterinary examination that no physical explanation of them exists, such as diabetes, thyroid disease, etc. Some experts suggest that bizarre appetites in otherwise healthy cats can be alleviated by increasing the amount of fibre, such as bran, in the diet or by giving the cat a gristly bone to chew on.

◀ **Increasing the time you spend with your cat can help prevent some obsessive-compulsive behaviours. Provide more opportunities and toys for hunting-related play.**

◀ Cats can display obsessive-compulsive behaviours such as chasing their tails.

◀ Many cats enjoy playing with balls of string, but some chew wool and string and you should take care that you do not leave your pet unattended.

Straying and leaving home

Even seemingly happy, contented and cherished cats do sometimes go missing. They may slip out of the cat flap one day and not return. We do not own our cats and if we give them free access to the outside world, they may sometimes go AWOL.

Moving house

The commonest reason for a cat running away is when its family moves house. Being highly territorial by nature, the animal is attempting to return to its old, familiar haunts. Lost cats frequently succeed in tracking down their old homes, often travelling over incredibly long distances. The longest recorded journey by a cat is 950 miles – from Boston to Chicago.

It is therefore important to keep a cat that is moved to a new house indoors for at least two weeks. After that it can gradually be let out under supervision and just before mealtimes, so that it will be keen to return inside after it has exercised. Make a point of bringing some of the cat's bedding and possessions from the old house when you move to enable it to identify with its own personal scent.

▲ Most cats will always return to their own home for food at regular mealtimes. If you move house, only let your cat out when it is hungry before you usually feed it.

Indoor cats

Permanent indoor cats can disappear when a door or window is accidentally left open. Inquisitive about and fascinated by the world outside, they leave the house and at once find themselves in strange, foreign and possibly frightening territory. They may hear unfamiliar noises or come face-to-face with next-door's dog or hissing tom. Scared, they run to some hiding place, such as a neighbour's garage, only to get locked in. Timid-natured cats may be too frightened by their experience to come out, even when they hear their owner searching and calling for them.

▶ Cats may take time to adapt to a new garden and surroundings if you move house. Give your pet the opportunity to settle in to its new home and acclimatize.

Butter paws

I'm afraid that the idea of putting butter on a cat's paws to prevent it from straying is nothing but a rather curious old wives' tale.

◄ Most cats would not
dream of leaving home
and all their usual
comforts. However,
even contented
ones can sometimes
disappear for no
apparent reason.

Other reasons for absconding

Cats rarely run away from home because they have been ill treated. For these animals, it seems that home territory is more important than home unhappiness. Perhaps surprisingly, excessive interaction by loving owners can sometimes drive a cat away. To encourage your pet to come more often to you looking for attention, don't over-fuss your cat.

A cat may decide to pack its bags and leave home if it is experiencing difficulties integrating with the neighbourhood cats. This is not an easy problem to solve, but you could try discussing matters with the neighbours who own the problem cat. If you are lucky, you might be able to agree on a timetable governing the times at which your respective cats are let out. A new cat, dog or human baby in the family can also be upsetting for a cat. Make sure you give it plenty of attention and lots of quality play-time.

Another cause of Puss absconding can be illness or injury. Sick or in pain, the cat seeks out somewhere under cover where it can hide away and wait until, hopefully, it feels better.

see also...

Olfactory communication
pages 64–65

Moving house
page 123

Elderly cats
pages 124–125

CHAPTER FIVE

A healthy lifestyle

The cat's elegant, tough body design goes some way towards confirming the traditional belief that cats have nine lives. However, its inquisitiveness and closeness to the ground expose it to a broad spectrum of germs, and stress or poor condition can lower its resistance to disease. By doing everything possible to maximize their pet's potential for a healthy lifestyle, responsible owners can help to prevent some common feline health problems occurring and also make their cats more contented.

Health essentials

To keep your cat fit and healthy you need, as a responsible owner, to supervise the different aspects of its lifestyle and environment. By feeding a healthy diet, grooming on a regular basis and providing plenty of opportunities for physical exercise and mental stimulation, you can actively promote your pet's wellbeing.

Diet

Nowadays, it is easy to feed a cat on a variety of proprietary foods in cans or packets but are these foods adequate for the bodily needs of your cat? And what are the alternatives? Whether your cat is a fearless outdoor hunter or a fireside house cat, you need to provide a nutritionally balanced healthy diet.

Exercise

Cats, far more than dogs, are self-exercising – you don't have to take them for walks. Nevertheless, encouraging game-playing with your pet and providing the opportunity for it to climb, run and jump in its environment will permit it to bring its muscles and tendons into use, polish up its reflexes and keep its heart action and blood circulation in good condition.

Feline addictions

Unfortunately, some cats do fall victim to the human vice of alcoholism. Jack, a black tom cat from Brooklyn, New York, was said to have given up drinking water at the tender age of three, preferring milk laced with Pernod. As he grew older, he demanded increasingly stiffer saucers of 'milk' until it was a question of lacing the Pernod lightly with milk. Jack gave up the ghost when he was eight years old, and, not surprisingly, a post-mortem found his liver to be in a sorry state.

▶ Free-roaming cats with access to a garden and beyond will take their exercise without their owners being involved.

Natural behaviour

Your cat should be permitted and encouraged to indulge in its natural feline behaviour. Wherever possible, it should be allowed out, ideally via a cat flap, to explore the world around its home. It needs to chew grass and plants in the garden (provided any fertilizer you use is not toxic), do some climbing, running and jumping, and, hopefully, make social contact with other cats in the neighbourhood.

Health checks

Although you will take your pet to the vet if you believe it to be ill or afflicted in any way, it is essential that you check it over yourself on a regular basis, say, once a week, to look for emerging signs of trouble. It is easy to do: with the cat sitting on your lap, inspect its ears, eyes, mouth, legs and skin, looking for any telltale signs of poor health or anything abnormal.

◀ **Check your cat for telltale signs of ill health when you spend some quiet time together.**

▼ **Most cats enjoy playing games with toys, and you should provide a range of stimuli for your pet.**

A healthy diet

All cats are carnivores and they must have meat in some form to survive, but this does not mean that they don't like or need to eat some vegetable matter or fruit. Wild big cats, such as lions and tigers, often go straight for their victim's stomach after making a kill, devouring the soup of digesting vegetation as a first course, before progressing to the main course of prime fillet or porterhouse.

A varied menu

Variety is the key principle to observe when you are feeding your cat. You should accustom a kitten to a wide variety of food from the day it is weaned.

Although pet cats should have a diet that is at least 25 per cent protein, they ought to follow their wild cousins and eat a varied menu that contains a little vegetable matter as well as the staple meat and fish. Providing fats and carbohydrates in your cat's diet as sources of energy makes good sense as, to an extent, an all-protein diet of meat or fish is wasted. This is because some of the expensive foodstuff is simply burned by the cat's body to provide calories instead of being used to repair cells.

Another reason for not feeding an all-protein diet is that it can be unhealthy. A cat fed on nothing but fish can develop vitamin B1 deficiency; a liver-only menu can upset its bowels; and a diet of nothing but prime lean meat produces calcium and vitamin deficiencies.

Did you know?

A cat can survive without food for much longer than humans as it can lose as much as 40 per cent of its body weight without dying. Cats have been known to survive for weeks without food or water in exceptional circumstances.

Chips, a marmalade tom from Liverpool, was inadvertently packed into a crate of machine parts and shipped by sea to Mombasa. Four weeks later, when the crate was opened in Africa, Chips was still alive, although somewhat thinner. He was thought to have survived by eating some of the grease coating the machinery and lapping up what little moisture developed from condensation.

◀ **Develop a routine that suits you and your cat and feed it at the same times every day. Your pet will get accustomed to this and will remind you that it's meal time if you forget.**

Liquids

These are essential to feline health, although a cat can survive with a lower fluid intake than us in proportion to its body size. An animal on a rich protein diet will produce plenty of urea and therefore will need a good volume of water to flush this waste product away via the kidneys. So do cats need a larger quantity of water for their size than we do? No, in fact they need less because they are able to produce a far higher concentration of urea in their urine than we can (almost three times as strong) and this helps them to conserve water. Nevertheless, fresh, clean water must always be available for your pet.

Milk is more of a food than a liquid for a cat. Its principal value is as a valuable source of calcium and phosphorus – a 200ml serving will provide an adult cat's daily needs. Some cats, however, cannot tolerate cows' milk and develop diarrhoea after drinking it. In severe cases, their diet should be modified to exclude milk, milk products and most cereal products. If this is the case, calcium supplements may be necessary. In mild cases, just dilute the milk with water.

▼ **Some cats can be quite fussy eaters but they may enjoy a smorgasbord of different tempting foods to stimulate their appetite and add variety to their everyday diet.**

Feeding guide

As with us human beings, a cat's nutritional requirements are for a regular, balanced supply of various foodstuffs. As a responsible owner, you should ensure that your pet eats a healthy and nutritionally balanced diet every day.

Protein

● A kitten requires 35 to 40 per cent by weight of its total diet daily in the form of protein.
● An adult requires 25 per cent by weight of its total daily diet as protein. Protein sources are meat, fish, eggs, cheese and milk. Note that a cat needs much more than a dog (13 per cent).

Planning your cat's meals

Age	Meals per day	Daily amount (g)
Weaning to 3 months	4–6	80–190
4–5 months	4–5	275
6–7 months	3–4	370
Over 9 months	2–3	400
Pregnant queens	3–5	420–460
Senior citizens	3–6	300–370

Fat

The daily fat requirement for a cat is 25 to 30 per cent of the total diet – again, more than that of a dog (5 to 10 per cent). Fats are a key source of calories for the cat, and because they do not load the kidneys with waste products, you should increase the fat content of your cat's diet as it gets older.

The principal sources of fat for your pet are meat and fish, especially oily fish. Contrary to what many people think, milk is not an important source of fat for cats nor is it, unlike water, an essential part of their diet.

Carbohydrate

The carbohydrate requirement, which is obtained from potatoes, cereals and bread, is up to 33 per cent of a cat's total diet. Although not essential, the associated fibre is good for bowel function and therefore many owners include some in their pet's diet.

▶ You can buy special proprietary foods for kittens, which supply all the essential nutrients they need for healthy development and growth in the first few months.

Vitamins

These are important elements in your pet's daily diet.
- Vitamins A and D occur naturally in milk, egg, liver, cod liver oil and carrots. Vitamin D is also produced by the effect of sunlight on the animal's coat. Overdosing is dangerous, so don't give your cat supplements.
- Vitamins B2, B6, biotin and folic acid are found in meat, liver, yeast and green vegetables, and some is also synthesized in the cat's intestine.
- Vitamin E is obtained from some meat and cereals.
- Vitamins C and K are actually produced in adequate amounts by chemical activity within the animal's body.

Note: Cats do not need Vitamin B12. Minerals and trace elements come from a balanced diet – an overdose can be dangerous.

Water

The daily amount of water that is needed by a cat is on average 30ml (six teaspoons) per 0.5kg of body weight. You should always make sure that an accessible bowl of clean, fresh water is available for your pet.

Give your cat a varied diet

Ring the changes frequently to keep your cat's diet interesting. Let's look at the major foods available. When composing your cat's diet, you should give two parts by weight of a selection of protein foods to one part of a selection of filler foods.

Protein foods

- **Manufactured:** May be dried, canned or soft-moist. Formulated to provide balance; no cooking required and therefore very convenient.
- **Meat:** Beef, lamb or pork. Bake or grill, then cut into small cubes. Do not buy from a knacker's yard.
- **Offal:** Must always be cooked. Do not buy offal from a knacker's yard.
- **Poultry and rabbit:** Feed cooked scraps but not bones. Pick them over carefully before feeding.
- **Egg:** Serve whole, cooked and chopped. Raw separated yolks can be fed but never feed raw egg whites or give more than two whole eggs a week.
- **Milk:** Pour it from the bottle. Note that some cats get upset stomachs on cow's milk but will tolerate soya or goat's milk. However, milk is not essential and your cat will thrive on water.
- **Cheese:** Serve a little cheese either raw and grated or cooked with other foods.
- **Fish:** Serve fresh and raw, steamed or grilled. If larger than a herring, chop and bone it. Canned fish in

tomato or oil can be given. Oily fish helps to dispel fur balls. Note that a diet of nothing but fish is unbalanced.

Filler foods

- **Vegetables:** Add cooked to meat or fish but no more than one-third of the meal.
- **Starchy foods:** Crumbled toast, pasta or potato can be mixed with gravy or fish stock. Cereal can be used with milk. Again, they should not make up more than one-third of a meal.

Feeding methods

It has been calculated that the daily requirement of a cat on a diet such as canned food that contains 25 per cent protein is 14g food per 450g body weight. The total daily serving required varies at different ages. Unlike dogs, cats are very similar in size and energy expenditure. Consequently, only age is a principal consideration in calculating feeding quantities. Although at one time it was thought that the ordinary overweight fireside pet did not need to slim, we now know that obesity is causing health problems, such as diabetes, in these animals.

▲ **A healthy cat should have a good appetite and enjoy its food, but take care not to over-feed your pet as this can lead to obesity and associated health problems.**

Grooming your cat

Cats are fastidious in keeping themselves clean, neat and well turned-out. However, although they devote a good part of their day to grooming themselves, they still need a little extra help from their owners, especially the longhaired varieties.

Functions of grooming

The importance of grooming is more than simply keeping the coat soft, glossy and clean. It has other functions, too – it removes dead hair and skin, tones up the muscles and stimulates the blood circulation. This explains why a mother cat cleans her newly born kittens so frequently. The maternal licking has the effect of stimulating the bodily functions of the youngsters. After a few weeks, with the mother's help, a kitten soon learns how to keep itself clean.

Pre-grooming health check

Before you start a grooming session, check your cat's ears, eyes, mouth and claws for cleanliness and any telltale signs of health problems.

● **Ears:** If necessary, clean out the ears with a piece of cotton wool dipped in olive oil.

● **Eyes:** Longhaired cats are prone to blockages of the tear ducts that result in tears running down the cat's cheeks and leaving unsightly dark marks. To remove these, gently wipe the animal's face with cotton wool dipped in a mild salt solution.

● **Teeth:** Examine the mouth and, ideally, clean your pet's teeth once a week with a soft toothbrush, salt and water or a specially formulated cat toothpaste.

● **Claws:** If the claws need trimming, hold the cat firmly in your lap and press the pad of its paw with your finger to make the claws come forward. Examine the claw carefully – the main part includes the pinkish-coloured quick containing the nerves. You must not cut this. The white tips are dead tissue; cutting this will not hurt the cat. If in doubt, ask your vet to it for you.

Grooming a shorthair

You will need the following grooming equipment: a fine-toothed metal comb, a soft natural bristle or rubber brush, some bay rum conditioner to rub into the coat (suits all coat colours) and a velvet, silk or chamois leather cloth for polishing the coat.

How often?

A shorthaired cat does not need daily grooming, as its coat is much easier to manage than that of a longhaired type. Moreover, shorthairs have longer tongues than their longhaired cousins and so are more efficient self-groomers. Two half-hour grooming sessions per week are therefore ample. In fact, some people believe that if you groom a shorthair more than twice a week it may stop grooming itself altogether.

Method

1 With the fine-toothed comb, work down the cat from its head to its tail. As you comb, watch out for any black, shiny specks – a sign of fleas.

2 Use a rubber brush to brush along the lie of the hair. If your cat is Rex-coated, this brush is essential as it won't scratch the skin. With some other shorthairs you may prefer to use a natural bristle brush.

3 After brushing and combing, if wished, rub in some bay rum conditioner to remove any grease from the coat and bring out the brilliance of its colour.

4 Finally, to bring out the natural glossy quality of the cat's coat, 'polish' it with a piece of velvet, silk or chamois leather cloth.

◀ Shorthaired cats only need minimal grooming, unlike their longhaired cousins. Most cats enjoy the attention and will happily allow their owner to fuss over them.

Grooming a longhair

For grooming a longhair you will need a wide and fine-toothed comb, a bristle and wire brush for the coat, a toothbrush, some blunt-ended scissors to cut out any mats, and some bay rum conditioner for dark cats or talcum powder for light cats to rub into the fur. For a show cat, you will also need a slicker brush to groom the tail.

How often?

In the wild, a longhaired cat would moult in the winter only, but because domestic cats are kept in artificially lit and heated conditions, they moult all year round. As a result, most longhairs need will daily grooming – two 15- to 30-minute sessions – otherwise their coats will matt. If matted balls of fur are not dealt with at an early stage, they will become painful and create a perfect environment for parasites and the development of inflammatory skin disease, and you will have to get a vet to shave them off while the cat is under general anaesthetic.

▼ Cats get accustomed to being groomed and most enjoy this quiet time with their owners. If you cat is free-roaming, take special care to look for any signs of fleas.

Make bathtime easier

If you think your cat is going to struggle when bathed, put it in a cotton sack with only the head visible. Pour shampoo into the sack and lower the cat and sack into the water. Massage the cat through the sack to form a lather.

Bathing a cat

If your cat's fur gets really dirty or greasy, bathing may be necessary. The kitchen sink makes the best bath. Make sure all the doors and windows are closed before you start and place a rubber mat in the sink to stop the cat slipping. The water in the sink should be about 5–10cm deep and at about 38.6°C.

1 Lift the cat into the sink by putting one hand under its rump and holding the scruff of its neck with the other.

2 Using a sponge, wet all the cat's fur except for its head. Next, rub a non-toxic cat or baby shampoo into the fur to produce a lather.

3 Rinse thoroughly with warm water to remove all the shampoo.

4 Lift the cat out of the sink and wrap it in a warm towel.

5 Now wash its face with cotton wool dipped in warm water.

6 Once the fur is dry, comb it gently. Dry the cat with the towel, keeping it in a warm place until it is totally dry. If it is not afraid of hairdryers, you can use one on a low setting, taking care not to singe the coat. Once the fur is completely dry, comb it through gently.

Method

1 With the wide-toothed comb, remove any debris and tease out any mats. Then change to the fine-toothed comb and go over the coat again.

2 With the wire brush, remove all dead hair. Pay particular attention to the rump, where you will probably be able to brush it out by the handful.

3 Brush some talcum powder or fuller's earth into the coat and brush out immediately.

4 Run the fine-toothed comb through the hair in an upwards movement, brushing the hair around the neck to form a ruff.

5 With the toothbrush, gently brush the shorter hairs on the cat's face. Be careful not to get too close to its eyes.

6 Finally, repeat step 4 with the wide-toothed comb to separate the hair and help it stand up. For show cats, use the slicker brush to fluff out the tail.

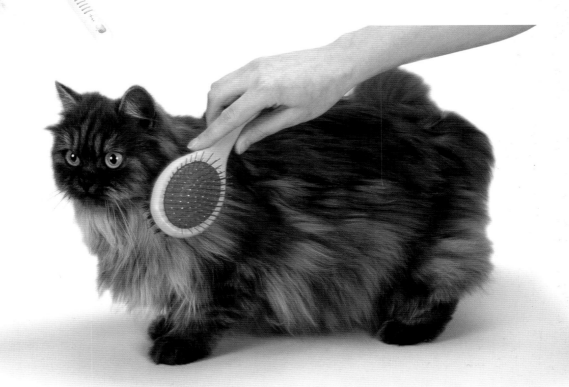

▶ **A wire brush is used to remove all the dead hair from the cat's coat.**

▲ **You will need to buy a selection of grooming tools, depending on your cat's coat, including soft and wire brushes, a rubber slicker and a fine- or wide-toothed comb.**

▶ **You need to use a combination of soft and stiff brushes for a longhaired cat to keep the coat in condition and free of knots and tangles.**

Health checks

You should check your cat for any tell-tale signs of potential health problems on a regular basis; prevention is always better than treatment. A good time to do this is when your pet is relaxed and sitting contentedly on your lap or by your side.

Ears

These must be kept free of wax, grease and scale. Clean them out gently with a cotton wool ball impregnated with a little olive oil, but if they have a tendency to become contaminated or clogged up again quite quickly, you should consider applying mite-killing ear drops (available from pet shops) or consult your vet.

The signs of ear trouble in the cat include the following:
● Shaking or scratching the head repeatedly
● Discharge visible in the ear canal that may be brown, purulent yellow, green or even blood-tinged
● A most unpleasant smell.

Problems begin when ear mites – minute parasites that are barely visible to the naked eye – invade the cat's outer ears. Their activities in sucking fluid from the ear lining cause irritation or pain, stimulate the accumulation of excess wax and scales and encourage secondary bacterial infection. Depending on the stage reached, treatment may involve anti-parasitic ear drops with or without antibiotics as well as thorough cleaning of the affected ear. Prevention is the key: routine checking and gentle cleaning, as described above, on a regular basis.

▲ You can use an ear-cleaning fluid to clean your cat's ears. These are available from your vet or most pet stores. A dab of olive oil on some cotton wool is a good alternative.

▲ Some cats may get discolouration of the fur under the eyes. You can clean this by wiping it away gently with some cotton wool soaked in a little warm water.

Eyes

Healthy eyes should be bright, clear and totally free of cloudiness and without any form of discharge. As part of your regular eye care for your cat, a couple of times each week, wipe the area around the eyes gently with some cotton wool dipped in warm water to remove any excess mucus. Eye problems are normally obvious and signs of trouble include the following:
● Cloudiness, usually white or bluish, of some or all of the transparent outer part of the eye (cornea)
● The smooth round surface of the cornea has a depression in it, perhaps indicating ulcer formation
● Apparent total or partial blindness when the cat bumps into things and loses its sense of orientation
● Sore, running, mattery eyes
● Blue-white cloudiness of the pupil of the eye
● Swollen eyelids
● The appearance of a small white membrane (the 'third eyelid', or nictitating membrane) in the inner corner of one or both eyelids.

Note: If any of the above symptoms occur, do not experiment with various home cures or pet shop eye-drops – see your vet as soon as possible.

Dental care

Examine your cat's mouth for any evidence of tartar build-up – a line of yellowish, crusty scale at the margins of the gums. Soft at first and hardening later, this deposit has a high calcium content and is mainly due to the milk and cereal elements of the cat's diet, the latter usually coming from the canned food it eats. One notable sign of your cat perhaps developing excess tartar is if its breath smells.

The main effect of an accumulation of tartar is on the gums rather than the teeth themselves. It encourages inflammation of the gums (gingivitis) and enables germs to enter the tooth socket. Slowly the infection creeps down the socket, creating periodontal disease. As a result, the tooth may become loose, the nerve will die and extraction will be necessary.

To prevent a build-up of tartar, you can clean your cat's teeth at least once a week with a soft toothbrush, water and salt or a specially formulated pet toothpaste (available from pet shops). In order to clean your cat's teeth effectively, you may need someone to help you.

Did you know?

Cats in the wild keep their teeth clean by chewing on raw food that automatically cleans up the mouth. Unlike our domestic cats, they tend not to suffer from tartar build-up.

Training a kitten

To train your kitten to scratch on a scratching post rather than on your Louis quinze escritoire, gently place its paws on the post until it gets the idea. Healthy kittens quickly get the message.

Ask them to press against the upper lips with their finger and thumb while you use your index finger to open the animal's mouth and expose the teeth.

Teeth cleaning may seem like an unnecessary chore but it only takes a few minutes and getting your cat accustomed to having its teeth cleaned from an early age will not only help to prolong dental health but will also prevent problems in old age.

Claws

Overgrown claws are understandably more of a problem for indoor cats that cannot wear them down naturally out of doors. Scratching posts and pyramids can help owners deal with this. It is very important to keep your cat's claws trimmed or they may grow round and embed themselves in the pad of the paw, causing pain and infection and necessitating veterinary attention. Special 'guillotine' clippers are better than scissors or even human-type nail clippers for this purpose. I have already described how to trim overgrown claws without damaging the so-called 'quick' (see page 100).

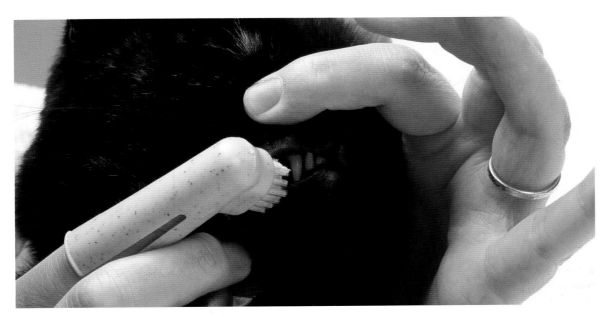

◄ **Brushing your cat's teeth with a soft-bristled toothbrush and veterinary toothpaste once or twice a week will help to prevent gum disease and bad breath.**

Exercise

As with us human beings, regular exercise is important for maintaining the good health and happiness of your cat. In recent years, there has been a noticeable increase in the number of cases of obesity in cats seen by veterinarians. The causes of this phenomenon – overfeeding and a sedentary lifestyle – are linked as very fat cats prefer to lie around. Gross obesity puts strains on the heart, liver and joints and can be a factor in the development of diabetes. No cat should weigh more than 8kg (17½lb).

Keeping your cat fit

Fortunately for those of us who are not fitness fanatics, unlike dogs, our cats do not need a daily five-mile hike. They can get sufficient exercise in their own garden, climbing trees, hunting birds and small rodents, chasing trespassing cats, dodging next door's dog and generally exploring their territory.

Lead walking

Unlike dogs, most cats do not enjoy walking on a lead, and only those cats with a suitable 'dog-like' temperament will accept it. Certain breeds, shorthairs rather than longhairs, take to it more readily than others; these include the Siamese, Burmese and Russian Blue.

Training a cat to walk on a lead is not easy and is best begun with a weaned kitten, which must first become accustomed to wearing a collar with an elastic insertion to act as a safety device if the pet gets caught, for example, in a branch when climbing a tree. Once the kitten is accustomed to wearing the collar, you can attach a long, thin lead or cord to it and start to walk

▶ **If you don't want to let your cat roam freely on its own outside, you could train it to walk on the lead. Some cats, such as this Burmese, enjoy lead walking.**

around, first in the house, then in the garden and later, perhaps, outside on the pavement. However, never drag a cat along on a lead against its will.

Indoor cats

These can keep fit by exercising on scratching posts and climbing frames. Regular play sessions and games with your cat are immensely beneficial. An hour or so of play each day is sufficient to maintain feline fitness and health. A rolled-up ball of tin foil or a ping-pong ball will keep your pet happily on the move. Encourage the cat to play with a toy from an early age and it will exercise itself and be more contented without any further effort on your part. If your circumstances are such that your pet has to be confined indoors permanently, do make sure that you select a breed that is suited to these living conditions rather than one that is renowned for its wanderlust, such as the Rex, Somali and Abyssinian.

You might also consider buying or even constructing a special enclosed outdoor run for your cat in the garden, perhaps linked to the house with access through a cat flap. Such runs may contain special exercise stations and scratching posts to keep a cat busy and well exercised and prevent boredom.

▲ **Many cats like to climb trees and survey the world from a high vantage point. This is normal behaviour and not to be discouraged.**

Did you know?

Cats, like humans, are either left- or right-'handed' or, I should say, 'pawed'. When using a forepaw to do something such as fishing a titbit out of a jar too small for its head, a male cat will favour its left paw whereas almost all females will favour their right one.

The importance of play

Like the young of other carnivores, kittens love to play – and it performs an extremely important function for them. Games serve as practice for independent adult life, not just amusement. Offensive and defensive roles, attack, pursuit, ambush and killing techniques are rehearsed in play, albeit on ping pong balls or cotton reels, but without carrying things too far or inflicting damage on their playmates.

Kittens

There is an air of excitement, exaggeration and bravura in the way that kittens play games, clearly showing that they enjoy fun for its own sake. Play also serves to develop a social sense and skills among cats. Kittens that are not able to play with others during their development period can grow up into rather anti-social, sometimes neurotic, adults.

You, the owner, must get involved in your pet's need to play. Have regular play sessions with your kitten every day for at least 15 minutes during which you roll small balls of tin foil for it to chase and retrieve, tease it with some little object on a string which you swirl about its

▲ **Brightly coloured objects on the end of a fishing line are always a hit with kittens and will keep them amused as they reach up to grab them or chase them along the floor.**

head and challenge it to intercept, or try indulging in a miniature tug o' war with you holding a strip of catnip-impregnated cloth while your kitten pulls against you with its teeth.

Adult cats

For adult domestic cats, as well as for wild cats kept in zoos, play relieves frustration and increases their contentment and interest in life. We regularly provide food for our pets without the need for a thrilling (and, in the wild, often fruitless) chase, so their powerful hunting instincts surface instead in the form of play. Playing games actually makes your cat more keen to eat, and what might otherwise be a monotonous and predictable meal becomes more fun.

▲ **All kittens love to play together. Sometimes they will lie in wait in a high place, ready to pounce or bat a playmate with a paw as they pass, unsuspecting , beneath.**

House cats

Cats that live entirely indoors can suffer from boredom, leading to them becoming sluggish or perhaps getting up to mischief. Therefore it is essential that they have a variety of playthings to distract them. Scratching posts are good, but even better are the climbing frames or play stations that are designed specially for cats and which you will find online or in the larger pet stores.

Suitable toys

Toys for a new kitten are equally important and you will find a wide variety on the market – take a look in your local pet store. Just as much fun for cats as bought-in manufactured toys, however, are cheaper household items, such as cardboard boxes, screwed-up balls of aluminium foil and old table tennis balls, which will all provide your cat with many hours of pleasure.

Do take care with items that have lengths of string attached. They will fascinate your pet but can result in dangerous entanglement. Never leave such toys lying around when no one is available to supervise your cat and play with him.

Games to play with your cat

Here are some simple ideas for games that you can enjoy playing with a kitten or an older cat.
● **The fishing rod:** Tie a soft toy or piece of cloth on to the end of a length of string attached to a stick. Either jiggle the 'bait' in the air or drag it along the floor. Your cat will eagerly 'hunt' it.
● **Hide and seek:** Show your cat something it really likes, such as a tasty treat or packet of its favourite food, and then try to hide. The cat will follow you everywhere and the fun is in seeing your pet tracking you down, usually successfully.
● Make a small hole in a cardboard box or stout paper bag. Point the open end of the box or bag towards your cat, then poke a long straw through the hole and move it about. Your cat will be quick to stalk it.
● If you have a laser pointer of the kind used in lectures, put out the lights and move the little dot of red light around the room. Your cat will be fascinated and persistent in trying to catch the dot. Do not, of course, point the laser directly at your pet.
● Move your hand about beneath a blanket. Your cat will pounce on it as excitedly as if it had located a real live mouse in the garden.

▲ Brightly coloured balls and other simple toys can provide a kitten withe many hours of fun, both chasing and stalking it. Get a variety of different toys for playing games.

see also...

Kittens
pages 115–117

Play and games
page 66

Veterinary checks
pages 134–135

CHAPTER SIX

Kittens to senior citizens

As kittens grow up, they go through fascinating periods of learning and development, changing from weak, defenceless animals when newly born to fully independent cats at around six months. The average life span of the domestic cat is about 15 years but it is not uncommon to find some individuals that pass this figure, although few achieve the ripe old age of 20. As a responsible owner, you should be aware of the changes wrought by the passing of time, as your playful kitten becomes a sexually active adolescent, and the avid tree-climber and intrpid hunter gradually comes to prefer the comforts and warmth of the fireside.

Handling your cat

If they are handled correctly, most cats love being picked up and cuddled by their owners. However, for a cat to enjoy being picked up it must not only feel comfortable and secure but should also trust you completely. Here's the correct way to do it.

Support the body firmly

Correct handling is particularly important with new kittens, as their small rib cages are very fragile and bruise easily. Never pick up a kitten by the scruff of its neck as a mother cat would. Instead, hold it gently but firmly, placing one hand around its stomach and the other under its hind legs before lifting it. Be sure to teach your children how to handle your kitten or cat correctly, so that they always support the body firmly.

Some cats are extremely nervous about being picked up, but frequent gentle handling will help get them accustomed to it. Socialization is also important and it is a good idea to ask your visitors to make a point of handling your kitten as this will help it to get used to the attentions of strangers.

Grown cats can be picked up with one hand around the stomach, just behind the front legs, and the other under the hindquarters. Once picked up, a cat will probably be happiest sitting in the crook of your arm, with its forepaws either leaning against your shoulder or held in your other hand.

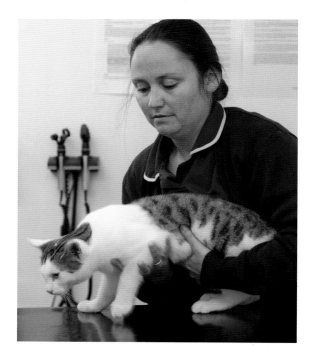

▲ To lift your cat or kitten, place one hand under its hind legs and the other around its stomach.

▲ Holding the cat firmly but gently, lift it up, hugging it into your chest. Bend your knees if lifting from the floor.

▲ Support the front and rear of the cat's body as shown but do not squeeze it too tightly or hold it too loosely.

Training your kitten

A properly domesticated kitten must learn certain basic behaviours. As an owner, it is your responsibility to train your pet to use its litter tray and, where installed, a cat flap. Most kittens, even very young ones, become toilet-trained quite quickly.

Toilet training

When the kitten first begins to eat solid foods, at three to four weeks of age, it can be introduced to toilet training, but your kitten will be older than that if you acquire it from a breeder. It is important to start toilet training it as soon as you bring it home.

Locate the litter tray in an easily reached but quiet spot, such as a utility room, and on a washable surface. Place the kitten in it frequently, particularly when it crouches with its tail raised, ready to urinate or defecate or, indeed, when it has begun to do so.

Problem solving

Never rub a kitten's nose in its urine or droppings when it relieves itself in the wrong place as, attracted by the scent, it will regard that area as its permanent toilet. Always clean such an area scrupulously to avoid repetition of the soiling. If your kitten will not use its litter tray, check that the tray is in a quiet place and that the litter is fresh. Sometimes cats do not like the feel or smell of a particular kind of litter, in which case try other brands until you find one that works.

▶ **Provide your kitten with a scratching post to prevent it sharpening its claws on your treasured furniture.**

Milestones in a kitten's development

Vision:	Eyes open at 8–20 days; eye colour changes to permanent shade at 12 weeks
Mobility:	Crawls at 16–20 days; walks at 21–25 days; runs at 4–5 weeks
Weaning:	Eats first solids at 3–4 weeks; fully weaned at 8 weeks
Training:	Starts toilet training at 3–4 weeks.
Teeth:	All milk teeth at 8 weeks; permanent teeth appear at 12–18 weeks
Learning:	Washing at 4–5 weeks; play begins at 4–5 weeks; starts practising hunting at 6–8 weeks
Registration:	Register pedigree kittens at 5 weeks
Veterinarian:	Discuss worming with vet at 3 weeks; first vaccination at 9 weeks; second vaccination at 12 weeks; spay females at 16 weeks; neuter males at 36 weeks
Independence:	Earliest age for leaving mother at 6–8 weeks; totally independent of mother at 6 months.

Cat flap training

If you want your cat to have the freedom to come and go as it pleases, then it is a good idea to install a cat flap in an outside door to your home.

Using a cat flap

Whichever type you choose it should be set no higher than 6cm (2in) from the base of the door so that the cat can step, rather than jump, through it. A flap must have a locking device as a precaution against unwelcome visitors. If your pet is female and calling, local toms will regard your cat flap as an invitation!

Some cats need no instruction in the art of using cat flaps, whilst others may require some encouragement. Start by opening the flap (securing it so that it cannot close) and allowing your kitten to investigate it. If you place some food on the other side, this may tempt the kitten to go through, but make sure the flap is firmly fastened and won't drop down and alarm the animal. At first, encourage it to come in through the flap rather than go out. Once your pet has stepped through, release

the flap and use a titbit to encourage it to step back, but this time help it to push the flap open. The majority of cats grasp the idea after only a few short training sessions of this kind, usually within less than a week.

Flaps for nervous cats

Magnetized or key-collar coded cat flaps are best as they permit only your cat to exit and enter the flap. These devices are valuable for rescue cats, which are frequently nervous, finding competition with more territorially aggressive, outdoor cats very intimidating.

▶ **Cats soon get the hang of using cat flaps to gain entry to the outside world and back into their home. Use a locking device to prevent any unwelcome visitors.**

The contented kitten

A variety of stimulating toys (see page 109) will help to keep your kitten contented and busy, particularly when it is left alone. Interacting with its owner is very important for a young cat, and training will reinforce this process and be enjoyable for both of you.

Basic training

You can begin basic training by teaching your kitten when to stay and come. It is best to start doing this when the cat is young, and it is important that any training does not involve compulsion but is reinforced by tasty food treats and abundant praise.

'Stay'

1 Put your kitten on a table and then sit down, so that your heads are on the same level.
2 Do not stare directly into the kitten's eyes but blink slowly to put it at ease. It will soon lose interest and will turn to move away, whereupon say its name followed by 'Stay'.
3 Put your hand, palm open, in front of his face, about 30cm (12in) away. If the kitten stops moving, you should promptly say 'Good' followed by its name and then offer it a treat. Repeat the process often.

'Come'

Once the kitten has mastered the 'Stay' command, the time has arrived to move on to 'Come'.
1 Put the kitten on the floor, give the 'Stay' command and then back away to a distance of about 2m (6ft) and stop.
2 Wait for a few seconds and then say 'Come', followed by the kitten's name. If it complies satisfactorily, give the treat reward and lots of praise.
3 Repeat the process but this time wait a little longer before giving the command.

▼ **Kittens enjoy playing with their littermates. This is part of their natural learning and socialization process. If you get two kittens, they will play together.**

Developing social skills

The transformation of a kitten from its blind and helpless newborn state to full independence takes about six months. During that time, its physical and mental abilities mature steadily. The kitten's instinctive inbuilt knowledge is progressively enhanced by a process of learning through observation, imitation and practice through play, initially with its littermates and later with its owners.

The importance of play

Play is the vehicle of the feline learning process – the life of the specialized natural hunter-killer is rehearsed and perfected in the theatre of the game. A lone, artificially reared kitten with no role models to copy and emulate will never learn much of the repertoire of feline hunting skills. What is not learnt during the formative first few weeks of life cannot be acquired later. Kittens that watch and are, in a real sense, taught by their mothers learn more quickly than they would by watching some unrelated adult.

It is therefore nothing to worry about when young kittens indulge in regular rough bouts of fighting. Although it may appear alarming to the onlooker, play 'combat' of this kind almost never results in any wounds or the loss of a single drop of blood. As well as refining physical and mental abilities that will serve the cat well in adult life, there is, quite obviously, lots of sheer fun in kittens' boisterous play. As with a human child, play with its peers increases a kitten's social skills and sociability. The kitten that is denied the opportunity of play is likely to grow up into a rather antisocial and insular adult.

▶ **Play is an important means for a kitten to develop its social and hunting skills. It will stalk a toy and try to 'kill' it as an adult cat hunts real prey, like birds or mice.**

You should encourage play and interaction by your kitten both with other cats in your household and also with neighbouring cats, provided the latter are not belligerent characters.

Socializing with people

In addition, it is important that your kitten learns to socialize with human beings. So many feral cats, which are suspicious and antipathetic towards people they come across, were denied this kind of relationship, however transient, when they were young. Talking to, playing with, cuddling, stroking and grooming your kitten from the outset are vital in bonding the two of you. You should get your cat accustomed also to being handled and fussed over by other family members, friends and visitors. Playing with your kitten and stimulating it mentally will help prevent many common behaviour problems.

Did you know?

Under normal circumstances, a kitten packs a lot of learning and physical growth into half a year, equivalent to around 10 years in the human life span. As with humans, a perfect feline upbringing can best be achieved in a family environment (normally a one-parent family in the case of the domestic cat). In raising a strong and sensible cat, there is nothing to equal the natural milk and constant attention of the queen, the endless games and competition with siblings, and the opportunities to learn from and inwardly digest the example of the mother and other sophisticated adult felines.

The adolescent cat

In adolescence, the cat reaches the peak of its physical development. It should by now be reasonably experienced in life with other cats and human beings, although it will still continue to learn. As with teenage humans, sex is now very much on the scene and you, as an owner, much like human parents with their children, will have to cope with all the various aspects of your cat's burgeoning sexuality in order to keep it happy and fit and your household free of feline problems.

Sexual awakening

Female cats (queens) become sexually mature at between seven and twelve months; for males (toms) it's a little later – at between 10 and 14 months. Some pedigree queens, such as the Siamese, may come into their first heat at six months of age whereas longhaired breeds usually start when they are much older. With most breeds, only one litter of kittens a year is advisable but so-called Foreign types, such as the Siamese, Havana, Tonkinese and the Rexes, can give birth every seven to eight months without suffering any ill-effects.

Feline heat (oestrus) cycles are seasonal and tend to start in January, peaking in March or April, June and September. Normally the queen has no cycles between October and December but there are exceptions. This seems to be governed by reduced light levels affecting the master gland of the body, the pituitary, via information transmitted by the eyes. This explains why cats kept indoors are less likely to have an inactive period. Within any phase, two to three two-week cycles occur with each oestrus lasting two to four days.

Recognizing the signs

The signs of a queen coming into heat are as follows:
● She will be more restless, fussy, affectionate and fawning than normal
● She will groom herself more than usual and there will be greatly increased rolling and rubbing of her body
● She is likely to emit rather strident howls. This is known as 'calling' and she is indeed calling – for a mate
● She will frequently adopt a characteristic mating posture with her front end flat on the floor and her rear end raised high in the air. She will begin peddling away furiously with her hind legs while her tail is flicked to one side. If you stroke her, she will crouch down very low.

Responsible ownership

When your queen reaches adolescence you must be prepared to cope with the consequences of her sexual status. Queens in heat attract the unwelcome attentions of neighbourhood toms and should not be let out of the house. Keep an eye on the cat flap in case some feline Casanova decides to pop in. If you do not want your queen to have kittens, arrange for her and any tom in the household to be neutered. If you plan to let her breed, wait until she has had two fully developed heat periods, to give her body time to become sufficiently developed to handle pregnancy and lactation.

Unless you are setting up a breeding stud, all pet toms should be castrated after they are nine months old. This safe, painless operation, carried out under general anaesthetic, reduces fighting and straying, eliminates the pungent smell of tomcat urine and also avoids unplanned and unwanted litters.

Did you know?

There is an alternative to spaying queens – the use of contraceptive medication to prevent or postpone oestrus. This comes in the form of long-acting 'depot' injections or tablets and can be prescribed by a vet. However, spaying is preferable to using a contraceptive except for the following short-term reasons: to give a pedigree breeding queen a rest between litters; to avoid oestrus at certain times; or to plan the arrival time of litters. There are several disadvantages to the contraceptive pill. It cannot be given to diabetic animals; if given over a long period, it may increase a tendency to uterine disease; and it may produce side effects, such as sluggish behaviour, increased appetite and undesirable weight gain.

◀ Cats keep their claws sharp by scratching them on trees and scratching posts. As they progress through adolescence to adulthood, they become more sexually aware.

The contented adult

The adolescent cat passes smoothly into adulthood. The well-socialized cat has by now learnt a lot and has established its daily routine as well as its likes and dislikes.

Good pet ownership

The contented animal goes outside on forays at certain times, sleeps in favourite quiet spots and looks forward to mealtimes, play, grooming and cuddle sessions with its owner. It is more confident, not least because its position in the neighbourhood feline hierarchy is now fixed – it knows the local gang. You will have learnt its idiosyncrasies and timetable, particularly if you have owned it since a kitten and played a major part in creating a happy life for it. The two of you will have progressively bonded – that is ideal pet ownership.

Adopting an adult cat

Of course, not everyone chooses to acquire a kitten and many people welcome adult cats into their homes. When choosing a pet, the attraction of a tiny, defenceless kitten is obvious, but it will demand your attention and will need to be trained and socialized. An adult cat is generally much easier to care for than a kitten. It will already be litter-trained and, because it is not so inquisitive, will be less accident-prone. It will probably be vaccinated and neutered and, provided it was adequately socialized

▶ **Many people do not have the time to train a kitten and they prefer to adopt an adult cat from a rescue centre. Take your time studying all the available cats.**

as a kitten, it will enjoy the company of people and often, but not always, other pet animals.

There are some potential disadvantages, however, in rescuing or taking on an adult cat. It may have been badly, even cruelly, treated in the past and be carrying psychological baggage in the form of behavioural problems. In addition, you may know little or nothing about its health history; it may not even be easy to determine its age. If, with its previous owners, it was allowed to go outdoors, you cannot expect to keep it as an indoor pet – that would be cruel.

Cat rescue organizations and humane clinics usually have a range of adult cats needing a good and loving home. If you want a rescue cat, ask the staff for advice and discuss your circumstances and preferences with them. Don't simply go by appearances. Many adult rescue cats have had a rough time but, nevertheless, they can be integrated into a household of caring, patient and understanding people and make loyal and affectionate family members.

Micro-chipping

All cats should be protected from getting lost by fitting them with an effective means of identification. The best method is to have your pet microchipped by your vet. The microchip is a tiny item of electronic wizardry, about the size of a grain of rice, which is injected under the cat's skin and stays there permanently. It contains a registration number that

Collars and name tags

It may be a good idea to fit a collar and name tag to your cat even if it is microchipped. Your neighbours will not possess microchip scanners, so the collar can come in useful if the cat gets lost locally. However, do make sure that the collar has a built-in elastic insert that allows the cat to escape if it becomes snagged on a tree branch or something similar.

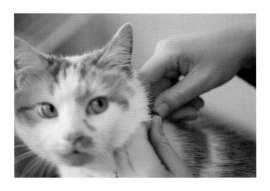

is specific to your cat alone and which can be read by a hand-held scanner. Vets, cat charities, police and border-control officers have these scanners. You will be given a record of the number and your vet will advise you on contacting organizations that trace lost pets, so that you can arrange for them to hold the number of your cat on their registers.

▼ **Microchipping (left) is a quick and painless procedure for the cat. The registration number on the chip can be read easily with a hand-held scanner (right).**

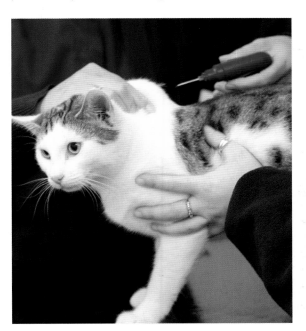

Travelling with your cat

Every cat owner should have a cat carrier, even for short journeys, to keep your pet secure. Most cats do not mind car travel but some get very nervous and stressed by the experience. Tranquillizers or sedatives may be prescribed by your vet for cats that are upset by travelling, as can other drugs for those affected by motion sickness.

High temperatures

In hot weather, you should not leave a cat for long periods in a closed car; even 10 minutes might be too long on a really hot day. Hyperthermia (over-heating) can occur remarkably rapidly, particularly in an excited and apprehensive animal, and may end fatally. Always park in a shady spot and make sure that a window is partially open if you leave your cat in a car on a summer's day for even the shortest period of time.

Going on holiday

At holiday time, most cat owners either arrange for a friend or neighbour to visit their pet in its own home each day or they take it to a boarding cattery. It is important to visit and inspect the cattery in advance of your departure and investigate the following:
● Are the boarded animals kept in separate accommodation out of direct contact with other cats?
● Are there snug, draught-free sleeping quarters as well as a reasonably spacious escape-proof outdoor run with equipment to keep your cat occupied?
● What are the feeding arrangements? Can you bring your pet's favourite food or do they already stock it?
● What are the arrangements if a cat falls ill? Who is their vet and does he/she make routine visits? If a cat falls ill, do they have a quarantine or hospital room if the vet considers it necessary?
● Must all the cats coming to be boarded have been vaccinated against panleucopenia (feline enteritis) and feline influenza and be accompanied by a valid vaccination certificate? If this is not the case, look for another cattery.
● If you are bringing more than one cat from your family, can they be kept together?
● Are the premises clean and in good condition? Do the staff appear efficient and caring?

Taking your cat abroad

Sometimes, cat lovers who own second homes overseas like to take their pet with them on holiday. If you fall into this category and want to take your cat

Pet Passports

There are some countries, including the European Union, from which cats can be imported into the UK without being quarantined provided they have a Pet Passport. To obtain this document, contact your vet at least eight months before your first intended journey abroad. Your pet will have to be micro-chipped, vaccinated against rabies and blood-tested afterwards to confirm that the vaccine has 'taken'. The animal has to be treated against parasites in a prescribed way before returning to the UK. Details of all this can be obtained from your vet or your local DEFRA office.

to a European Union or certain rabies-free qualifying countries, you will have to get a Pet Passport. For more information, talk to your vet and contact your local DEFRA office or look online at www.defra.gov.uk. It takes time to organize, so plan ahead and check out the requirements a few months before you travel.

This needs careful planning and you must be sure to familiarize yourself with the regulations governing importation of animals in your country of destination. Check with your travel agent, shipping agent, airline freight company or the embassy of the country that you intend visiting regarding quarantine, health certificates and transportation.

Air, rail and sea travel

If you intend to take your cat by plane, you must use a cat container that is approved by the International Air Transport Association (IATA). Some airlines have their own rules, so check before the flight. Before taking your cat to the airport you should do the following:

1 Give the animal a light meal and a drink two hours before despatch. However, do not feed it just before travelling or it may be sick in its carrier.

2 If your vet has recommended a tranquillizer, give it as directed or just before you hand the cat over. Some rail companies allow your pet to travel with you provided it is in a cat container but, again, check this in advance with the carrier. If your cat is travelling unaccompanied by sea, arrangements must be made for a crew member to provide daily attendance. Sea sickness, however, is rare in cats.

Moving house

Moving home does not usually trouble the family cat. It retains its well-loved human companions and normally many familiar items of furniture. After arriving at the new dwelling, the cat quickly sets about establishing

▲ **Cats take time to adapt to their new surroundings if you move house. Do not allow your cat to roam freely outside until it has settled in, and accompany it at first.**

its territory and leaves its calling cards of urine sprays, droppings and scratches for the attention of the feline patriarchs of the neighbourhood. Occasionally, perhaps longing for some old flame left behind or preferring the surroundings in which it grew up, a cat may even decide to trek back to its old haunts. As earlier described, it manages to do this principally by observing the angle of the sun.

Spoil and fuss over your cat during the first week in its new home, and play with it as often as possible. Keep it indoors for a few days but make sure you accompany it on its first outdoor exploration. Do not allow the newly arrived cat, even if it is an adult, to stay out at night.

The senior citizen

Nowadays, the average lifespan of a domestic cat is about 15 years, and although it is not uncommon to find individuals that live beyond this, few achieve the ripe old age of 20. The record stands for a tabby called 'Puss' who attained 36 years and one day, although there is an unsubstantiated claim that a cat lived to the age of 43.

The ageing process

As cats age, they change physically, frequently becoming thinner, and their appetite often alters – these changes may be due to a failing liver or kidneys. Constipation, caused by impaction of the large intestine and rectum, can occur in older cats, particularly fastidious self-groomers. Increased thirst and incontinence in the old cat may indicate the onset of diabetes or cystitis. Elderly cats can also suffer from arthritis and joint disease, although it is much less common in felines than in humans or dogs.

Vision

▼ Like humans, old cats grow weary and like to relax and take life easy. Many sleep more than in their youth, napping for up to 18 hours a day, and seeking out quiet spots.

Opacity of the pupil of the eye can be due to the development of a cataract in the lens and is particularly likely to occur in old cats with diabetes. Opacity of the lens in an elderly cat may also be merely a change in the refractive index of the lens due to age. This does not interfere with normal vision. Nevertheless, the old animal's eyesight and hearing may fail gradually. If this happens to your pet, remember that a deaf cat cannot hear potential dangers, such as the vacuum cleaner.

Owners of blind cats must keep their feeding bowls in the same place, avoid rearranging furniture and protect them from potential dangers, such as open fires.

Health checks

All elderly cats should receive regular check-ups with the vet once every three to four months. Regular veterinary attention throughout your cat's life should have prevented the build-up of tartar on its teeth, but a sudden fondness for soft snacks in later life may cause rapid tartar formation, gum damage, inflammation of the tooth sockets and loosening teeth. These, in turn, may contribute to kidney and liver rundown. Clean an elderly cat's teeth once or twice weekly.

Feeding tips

● If your elderly cat's appetite increases, give more food at each meal or offer more meals.
● Always provide high-quality protein food – fish, meat and poultry – and a variety of vegetables and fruit.
● Give warm water or milk as and when required – denying increased thirst is dangerous.

● You could try mixing one teaspoonful of lard with the cat's usual food to provide the extra calories needed by an old very lean animal.

● Try adding a few drops of mineral oil to your cat's diet occasionally to combat constipation.

● Feeding bran and oily fish can help ease constipation problems in elderly cats.

Dementia

In old age, some cats develop changes in the brain that are very similar to those found in people with Alzheimer's disease or dogs with canine cognitive dysfunction. There are a number of signs that indicate a pet may be suffering from dementia of this kind. They include loss of memory, forgetting locations of familiar things such as doors or litter trays, getting lost in the house it has lived in for years, aimless wandering, decreased activity, altered relationships (the cat wants more attention or becomes increasingly irritable and perhaps aggressive), reduced or increased appetite, changed sleeping patterns and less grooming.

It is your duty as a responsible owner to show both patience and understanding if this happens to your pet. Treatment is not easy but giving nutritional anti-oxidants, such as Vitamin E, may be helpful, and your vet may prescribe an anti-dementia medication.

▲ **Elderly cats are quite content to sit at home and relax or sleep. They need regular meals, grooming and lots of human attention to keep them healthy and happy.**

Feline versus human years

It is not easy to equate any particular time in a cat's life with the corresponding one in a human. The common practice of multiplying the cat's age by a figure (often quoted as seven) and saying that there is a human equivalent is not really satisfactory. The most accurate table of equivalent ages for man and cat would look something like the one below.

Cat (years)	Man (years)
1	16
2	24
3	28
4	32
8	48
12	64
15	76
20	96

see also...

Neutering
page 118

Feeding guide
pages 98–99

Vision and eyesight
page 46

CHAPTER SEVEN

Health care

The ailments of cats have been studied intensively by scientists and are now well understood by the veterinary profession. As a cat lover and owner, it is your responsibility to keep your cat fit and healthy, recognize the warning signs of potential health problems and thereby prevent any future illness. When it comes to treatment, there are certain things that you can tackle yourself, but essentially, the vet is your pet's best friend.

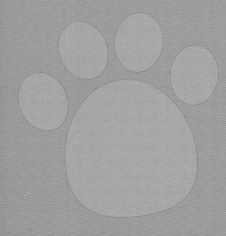

The healthy cat

The cat's elegant, tough body design might give some credence to the traditional belief that cats have nine lives. However, its natural inquisitiveness, closeness to the ground and ability to explore most nooks and crannies also expose it to all manner of germs. Its size predisposes it to certain types of accident, particularly if it is a city dweller, and stress or poor condition can lower its resistance, giving disease a chance to attack.

Signs of good health

So what are the features you will see in a healthy cat, hopefully one like yours? Here are some of the things you should look for in your pet:
- A healthy cat's fur is sleek and unbroken
- The eyes are clear and bright
- The nostrils are clean and dry, neither parched nor moist
- It has a good appetite
- Its excretory systems function regularly, as you can see from the litter tray or from its toilet activity outside in the garden
- It walks fluidly, moving with purpose and self-possession
- It grooms itself regularly with its tongue
- It purrs pleasingly at appropriate moments and does not show any sudden flashes of irritation or bizarre behaviour
- Lastly, handling by humans produces no signs of pain or discomfort.

Common signs of illness

The first signs of ill health that you will probably notice in your cat usually involve behaviour: it becomes duller, more introverted and less active. Also, its appetite is often affected and may decrease or increase. Here are some of the physical signs to watch out for:
- **Respiratory signs:** Sneezing, nasal discharge, coughing

Signs of poor health

Major signs:
- Looking off colour
- Vomiting
- Diarrhoea
- Abnormal breathing
- Bleeding
- Scratching.

Acute signs:
If your cat displays any of the following signs consult a vet immediately – collapse, vomiting repeatedly for more than 24 hours, diarrhoea for longer than 24 hours, troubled breathing, bleeding from an orifice, dilated pupils.

- **Oral/appetite signs:** Drooling, overeating, under-eating, increased thirst
- **Eye signs:** Discharge, cloudiness of the cornea, closed eyelids
- **Ear signs:** Discharge, irritation with and scratching at an ear or ears
- **Body signs:** Pain when touched, limping
- **Bowel/urinary signs:** Constipation, frequent urination, straining.

◀ This cat, out hunting in the garden, looks really fit and healthy, with sleek fur and clear, bright eyes. It is inquisitive, alert and interested in everything in its environment.

External parasites

Parasites living on the skin and amongst the fur of cats are quite common, and you should watch out for any telltale signs of them during grooming sessions. You can protect your pet by treating it regularly with preparations available from your vet.

Fleas

A cat can become infested with feline, dog or human fleas, and their presence can make the animal scratch, twitch or lick itself frenziedly. If you find particles that look like coal dust in your cat's coat, they are flea droppings. On the skin, small, reddish pimples with a darker, crumbly centre may develop, particularly along the spine, an area that is especially sensitive to the protein in flea saliva. Fleas may carry tapeworm larvae and they can also spread certain viral diseases.

Although fleas lay their eggs on the cat, they do not cement them to hairs like lice do with their 'nits' (see below). Consequently, the flea eggs fall off the cat's body and continue their development towards the point when they hatch, lying on carpets, furniture and, particularly, the cat's bed. There are special aerosols on the market that you can use on your pet's living areas to stop the eggs hatching.

Prevention: The best method is to use one of the veterinary aerosols containing methoprene or permethrin around the house once every six months.

Treatment: If your cat has fleas, use an anti-parasitic powder or aerosol, which is obtainable from a chemist or pet shop. Other modern anti-flea treatments available from your vet include injections, drops that are absorbed into the cat's body after being applied to the skin, and oral drugs that are mixed with the pet's food. Use them regularly to prevent infestations.

Ticks

Country-dwelling cats can sometimes pick up sheep ticks. These parasites suck blood, swelling up until they resemble blackcurrants. They don't move around as their mouthparts are buried securely in the cat's skin. For this reason, they should not be pulled off as the mouthpart may be left behind, later to cause an abcess.

▶ **Combing your cat's fur regularly with a special flea comb is helpful but it not a substitute for using effective anti-parasitic preparations in the form of sprays and capsules.**

Treatment: Remove ticks by applying a drop of chloroform or ether (if you have them) or one of the proprietary anti-parasite medications obtainable from pet shops and chemists. Wait until the mouth parts relax and then pick them off with tweezers, taking care not to leave the mouth parts buried in the cat's skin. Once you have removed the tick, treat the cat with an appropriate anti-parasitic preparation.

Lice

Two kinds of louse can sometimes be found on cats: a sucking type and a biting type. They can make their home anywhere on the body but the most common site is on the head. A heavily louse-infested cat will be run-down and anaemic.

Treatment: If you suspect that you cat has lice, you should consult your vet immediately, who will probably prescribe an anti-parasitic powder or drops.

Mites

Mange mites are minute creatures that burrow into a cat's skin, causing chronic inflammation, hair loss and irritation. The most common species found in cats is Notoedres, which affects the head and ear area, producing baldness, scurfiness and dermatitis.

Two other kinds of mite that are sometimes found on cats are the harvest mite, or chigger, which in autumn can cause irritation and areas of dermatitis on a cat's skin, and the fur mite, which may affect humans as well as furry pets, and causes excessive dandruff in the coat.

Treatment: If you find evidence of any of these parasites affecting your pet, seek professional advice from your vet or, if you are absolutely sure you can identify the little invader, use some form of medication in the form of anti-parasitic powders or systemically-acting pour-on drops.

◀ **Most vets agree that the best way to prevent fleas is to treat your pet cat regularly with anti-parasitic drops that are applied at the back of the head onto the cat's skin.**

Internal parasites

Many kinds of internal parasite can find a home in your cat in virtually any of its tissues, including the eyes, lungs and heart. The commonest feline internal parasites are worms of which the most important are the ones that invade the animal's gastro-intestinal tract – roundworms, tapeworms and flukes.

Roundworms

Two kinds of roundworm are commonly found in cats. They don't suck blood but feed on digesting food in the cat's intestinal canal. Eggs are laid which pass out in the stools and are then eaten by another cat, either directly, or after passing through mice, rats or beetles. Larval worms can even penetrate the placenta to infest the foetus in the womb, and they are sometimes present in the mother's milk. Once in a kitten's body, the worms migrate through the liver, heart and lungs to the intestine. Kittens are thus much more seriously affected than adults and may develop diarrhoea, constipation, anaemia, pot bellies or poor condition.

Whipworms and threadworms

These are rarer in cats than roundworms but, like the latter, have a direct life cycle, the eggs and larvae requiring no intermediate host. Threadworm larvae inhabit the small intestine where they burrow into the wall and may cause haemorrhages, whilst whipworms prefer the large intestine. External signs of both parasites include diarrhoea, weight loss and anaemia.

Hookworms

These serious blood-sucking worms enter their host via the mouth or by burrowing through the skin and then migrate to the small intestine. They can even pass through the placenta to unborn kittens. These worms produce diarrhoea (often blood-streaked), anaemia and weakness in infected animals.

Flukes

Found in the small intestine, pancreas and bile ducts, flukes are rare in British cats but relatively common in Europe, Asia and Canada. The intermediate hosts are a snail and a freshwater fish. Signs are digestive upsets, jaundice, diarrhoea and anaemia.

Worming tablets

Tablets for routine worming of the cat can be obtained from the pet shop or from your vet, but if you think that the animal is actually showing symptoms that may be parasite-related, you should make arrangements for a proper veterinary examination.

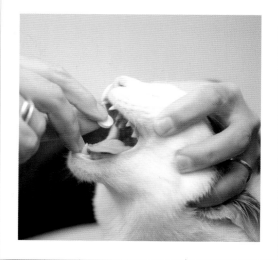

Toxoplasma

An important parasite that is not a worm but a microbe is Toxoplasma. The cat sheds the parasites in its stools and these can be passed to humans. Although rare, Toxoplasma infection is a risk to pregnant women and their foetuses. You can take the following precautions against catching it from cats:
1 Always wash your hands after touching a pet
2 Don't allow pregnant women or young children to come into contact with cat droppings – they should not handle cat litter
3 Cover children's sandpits to keep cats out of them when they are not in use.

Tapeworms

These live in the small and large intestines and share the cat's food without sucking blood. They may cause irritation and flatulence but little else. When segments of tapeworm pass out of the cat's anus they often stick to the rear end and resemble rice grains. The intermediate hosts of tapeworms are mice and fleas although one common US tapeworm has two intermediate hosts – first a tiny crustacean, then a fish.

▲ **Even young kittens need to be wormed regularly from six weeks of age and then once every two to three months; thereafter once every three to four months in adults.**

Seek professional advice

Always ask your vet for advice in treating your cat if you suspect that it is carrying parasites. Regular worming against tapeworms every four months and roundworms every six months is advisable.

Taking your cat to the vet

Apart from the times, hopefully only very infrequently, when a cat falls ill, you will not have to visit the vet very often. However, check-ups are advisable, especially for newly acquired pets, together with vaccinations and procedures such as neutering. Ideally, elderly cats should be examined by a vet once every three to four months.

At the clinic

I have already discussed the best way to transport your pet to the veterinary clinic. You must use some secure form of cat carrier and never take it 'loose'. Make a precisely timed appointment, if possible, and leave the cat in the car until it is your turn to go into the consulting room. You don't want your pet to be among other animals, some of which may be coughing or sneezing germs in a crowded waiting room, if it can be avoided. If a cat has become very frightened and perhaps aggressive during past visits to the clinic, the vet may prescribe a tranquillizer, such as Valium, to be given an hour before the appointment.

Vaccinations

It is important that every cat is vaccinated as early as possible against the dangerous feline viral diseases: cat flu, feline panleucopenia (also called feline enteritis) and feline leukaemia. In some countries and for cats that are transported internationally, the rabies vaccine is also administered, and a special vaccine against feline infectious peritonitis has been developed, although it is not available everywhere.

Your vet will advise on the most appropriate time to take a kitten for inoculation. Usually the vaccination course consists of two injections, three to four weeks

▶ **Most vets will advise giving your cat a booster vaccination on an annual basis, although opinions vary. If your cat is free-roaming and meets other felines, it's advisable.**

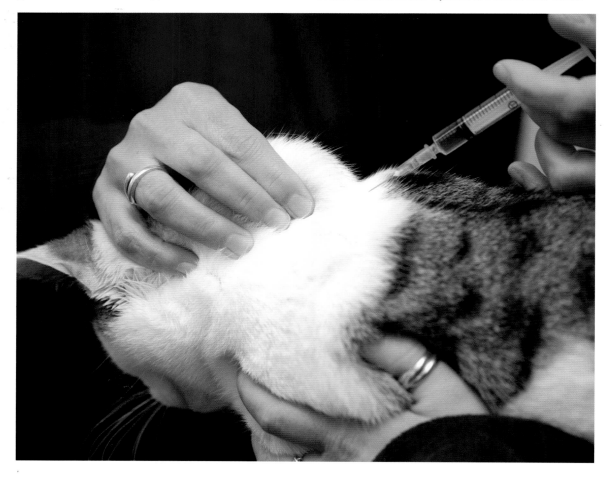

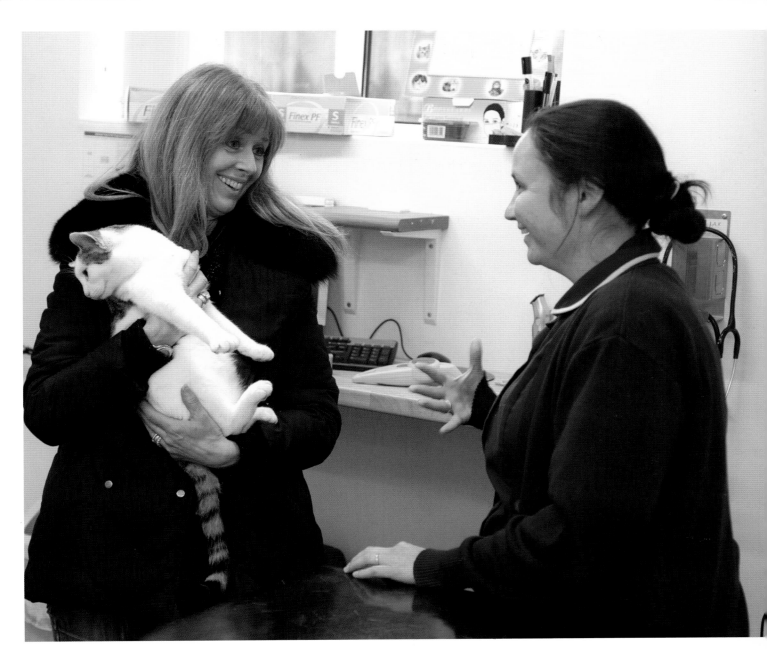

▲ Try to establish a good relationship with the staff at your local veterinary clinic, so they get to know you and your pet and visits are a more relaxing experience for the cat.

apart, with the first one at eight to nine weeks of age. After that a single booster dose of vaccine is given annually although there has been some debate among veterinary scientists recently as to whether this is essential. Vaccinations usually do not produce side effects, although there have been cases recorded of unpleasant reactions at the injection point of some feline leukaemia vaccines.

Cats can be vaccinated separately for cat flu, panleucopenia and feline leukaemia but the vet will usually use a three-in-one vaccine that protects against them all in a single injection. Rabies vaccine is always

a separate inoculation. It is vital that your cat is kept indoors and out of contact with the neighbourhood cats until two weeks after the first shot of vaccine. Your vet will give you a vaccination certificate, which you should keep in a safe place. Take it with you when your cat goes back to the clinic for its booster shots. More importantly, you can show it to the staff at the cattery if your pet is boarded there as proof of its up-to-date vaccination status.

Keeping your cat healthy

There are four principal ways by which you can reduce your cat's chances of becoming ill – taking basic hygiene precautions; registering your pet with a local vet; getting it vaccinated; and keeping it out of danger. Read the expert advice below.

▼ **When you acquire your cat, make sure you register it with a local vet. Don't wait until a problem arises; you may have difficulties getting an appointment.**

Basic hygiene

Hygiene is most important for preventing health problems, so do make sure that you keep your pet's bedding and feeding dishes scrupulously clean. Check its ears, eyes, nostrils, mouth, feet, fur, genitalia and anal area regularly to make sure that they are free from dirt, any discharge and abnormalities.

Registration

As soon as you acquire a cat, register it with a local vet, ideally one who specializes in the domestic cat or small animals. Such vets have premises equipped with facilities for the most up-to-date medical and surgical techniques. All vets are trained in feline diagnosis and treatment, but finding a vet who has a special

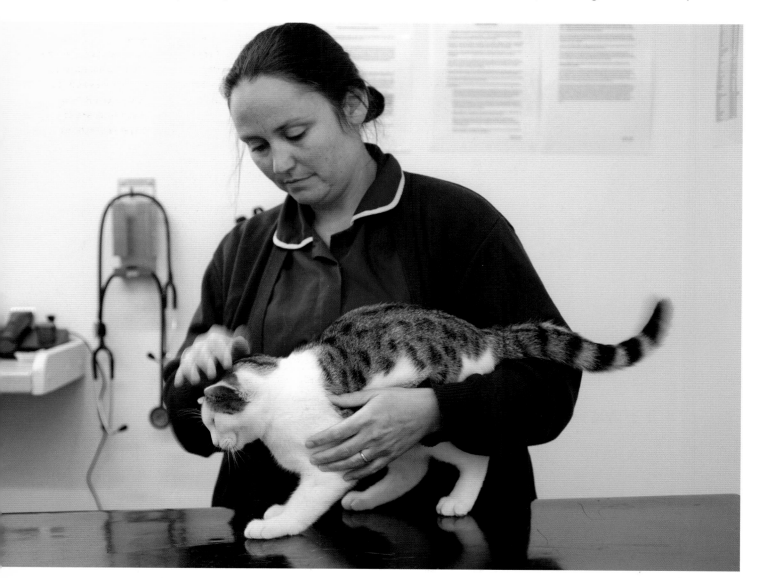

'feeling' for cats – who handles them with sympathy and interest, and who will explain a diagnosis clearly – is better than choosing a practice on the basis of advanced hardware and fancy surgical techniques. It is also worth considering joining a pet medical insurance scheme as this can ease the financial burden and worry of unexpected disease and accidents.

Vaccinations and parasites

Make sure your cat receives preventive vaccinations against the major infectious diseases (see page 134) and that it has booster doses at times advised by your vet. Also protect your pet against external and internal parasites by using anti-flea preparations and worming tablets on a regular basis. Ask your vet for advice.

Out of danger

Don't let your pet just go wandering far and wide, particularly if you live in a town near a busy road with heavy traffic. You can restrict your cat to your own garden by erecting some form of light netting and supervising its outdoor expeditions or even training it to walk on a lead. Check that your house and garden are cat-friendly and safe, especially regarding common poisons (see the table below).

Poisons

Cats are at risk from a number of poisons, which are ingested in two main ways: firstly, if a cat's coat becomes contaminated with a chemical, it will lick it off in an attempt to clean itself; and, secondly, its hunting lifestyle may lead to it eating, unwittingly, poisons that are used to kill pests in the garden.

If you suspect poisoning, contact your vet at once and arrange for an immediate examination. If you have time, wash the cat with human hair shampoo, rinse it well and dry it thoroughly. If you suspect that a particular chemical is causing the trouble, make sure you take a sample of it to the vet's.

Treatment

If indicated (see below) or on veterinary advice, give the cat an emetic to make it vomit, a demulcent to protect its stomach and intestines, or a laxative.
- **Emetic:** A pea-sized piece of sodium carbonate given as a tablet, or a very strong solution of salt in water or mustard in water.
- **Demulcent:** Milk, raw egg white, Milk of Magnesia or olive oil.
- **Laxative:** Mineral oil or magnesium sulphate.

▲ **If you acquire an adult cat, take it to the vet for a health check. it will need worming as well as anti-flea treatments and the usual vaccinations.**

Common poisons

TYPE	SOURCE	VISIBLE SIGNS	EMERGENCY ACTION
Arsenic	Horticultural sprays, rodent poisons	Vomiting, diarrhoea, paralysis	Wash coat, emetic
Lead	Paints	Paralysis, nervous signs	Wait for vet
Phosphorus, Thallium	Rodent poison	Vomiting, diarrhoea	Emetic
Phenols, Cresols	Wood preservative	Burnt mouth, vomiting	Wash coat, demulcents
Tar products, Turpentine	Tar	Convulsions, coma	Demulcents, particularly milk
Aspirin	Tablets	Vomiting, liver damage	Emetic, demulcent
Warfarin	Rodent poison	Stiffness, diarrhoea, haemorrhages	Wait for vet

Nursing a sick cat

Gentle, loving attention from its owner is essential in nursing a sick cat back to health. Nursing, in its broadest sense, is as important as all the pills and potions in the world.

Rest and warmth

The main requirements of a sick cat are rest and warmth. Good draught-free ventilation is important if your pet has a respiratory ailment. Warmth can be provided by background central heating, a fan heater, infra-red lamps, a hot water bottle or blankets. Take care if using infra-red lamps or hot water bottles – they can cause burns if placed too close to the patient. Set up and turn on a lamp, wait a minute or two, then test the distance – usually a minimum of 60cm (24in) – by placing your hand where the cat will lie. Hot water bottles are best wrapped in a cloth cover.

Appetite loss and dehydration

Although loss of appetite is a common feature of many feline illnesses, cats rarely die from starvation even after many days without solid food. However, you must guard against dehydration. This can be caused by a drastic reduction in fluid intake, perhaps aggravated by diarrhoea or vomiting, and can kill a cat very quickly.

Taking tablets

Giving a cat a pill or tablet generally requires two people: one immobilizing the animal by pressing it down firmly onto a flat surface with one hand on its scruff, while the other person acts a 'pill pusher'. If your cat is not cooperative, wrap it in a towel first with only the head protruding.
1 The 'pill pusher' grasps the head from above and gently tips it back, placing their index finger and thumb where the jaws meet.
2 Press the lips in as the mouth opens slightly and then, with the other index finger, push the lower jaw down and drop the pill far back on the tongue.
3 A quick push with a finger or the blunt end of a pencil should send the pill over the back of the tongue.

Nursing guidelines

● Don't crush tablets and sprinkle the resulting powder onto the cat's tongue as many drugs have an unpleasant or bitter taste, which will cause the animal to produce copious, foamy saliva and become agitated.
● Similarly, liquid medicines are often bitter and may induce salivation. The easiest way of giving these is by spoon-feeding (see box left).
● Mixing medicines with your pet's food is not a good idea. Most cats will detect the drugs and refuse to eat.

Spoon feeding

You should provide nourishing liquid food if needed, spoon-feeding one to three teaspoons of glucose and water, beef tea or proprietary liquid invalid foods as often as possible.
1 Grasp the cat by its scruff and twist your wrist so that its head is flexed back and the mouth opens.
2 Spoon in the liquid, drop by drop, letting it run down the tongue. Let the cat swallow after every 2–3 drops or it may choke.

Feline essentials

During your cat's illness, it is especially important to continue with your regular hygiene, grooming and inspection routines.

▶ **To keep a sick cat warm, you can wrap a hot water bottle in a snug cover and place it next to the affected animal.**

◄ To keep a sick cat warm, you can wrap a hot water bottle in a snug cover and place it next to the affected animal.

see also...

Going on holiday
page 122

Health checks
pages 104–105

Grooming
pages 100–103

Useful information

Animal Samaritans
Registered charity that rescues and rehomes unwanted and ill-treated pets.
PO Box 154
Bexleyheath
Kent DA16 2WS
Tel: 020 8303 1859
www.animalsamaritans.org.uk

Association of Pet Behaviour Counsellors
International network of qualified counsellors treating behaviour problems in pets.
PO Box 46
Worcester WR8 9YS
Tel: 01386 751151
www.apbc.org.uk

Animal Health Trust
Animal welfare charity focusing on health and providing genetic testing and specialist veterinary care.
Lanwades Park
Kentford
Newmarket
Suffolk CB8 7UU
Tel: 01638 751000
www.aht.org.uk

Battersea Dogs' Home
Rescue centre for pets, offering rehabilitation and homing.
4 Battersea Park Road
London SW8 4AA
Tel: 020 7622 3626
www.dogshome.org

Blue Cross
Animal welfare charity with animal hospital and adoption services.
Shilton Road
Burford
Oxon OX18 4PF
Tel: 01993 822651
www.bluecross.org.uk

British Veterinary Association
Governing body of the British veterinary profession.
7 Mansfield Street
London W1G 9NQ
Tel: 020 7636 6541
www.bva.co.uk

Cat World (magazine)
Ancient Lights
19 River Road
Arundel
West Sussex BN18 9EY
Tel; 01903 884988
www.catworld.co.uk

Cats Protection
UK national charity seeking to promote responsible cat ownership, and rescuing and rehoming unwanted and abandoned cats.
National Cat Centre
Chelwood Gate
Sussex RH17 7TT
Tel: 08707 708649
Helpline: 03000 12 12 12
www.cats.org.uk

Celia Hammond Animal Trust UK
Rescue and rehoming shelters for unwanted and abused pets.
High Street
Wadhurst
East Sussex TN5 6AG
Tel: 01892 783367
www.celiahammond.org

Cinnamon Trust
Charity providing benefits to the wellbeing of elderly pet owners.
10 Market Square
Hayle
Cornwall TR27 4HE
Tel: 01736 757900
www.cinnamon.org.uk

The Feline Advisory Bureau
Charity that promotes cat health and welfare through improved feline knowledge.
Taeselbury
High Street
Salisbury
Wiltshire SP3 6LD
Tel: 01747 871872
www.fabcats.org

The Governing Council of the Cat Fancy
Governing body for pedigree cats in the UK.
5 King's Castle Business Park

The Drove
Bridgwater
Somerset TA6 4AG
Tel: 01278 427575
www.gccfcats.org

The Mayhew Animal Home
Provides advice, care and assistance to pet owners, plus rehabilitation and rehoming services.
Trenmar Gardens
Kensal Green
London NW10 6BJ
Tel: 0208 969 0178
www.mayhewanimalhome.org

National Animal Welfare Trust
Rescue centres for rehoming unwanted pets.
Tyler's Way
Watford By-Pass
Watford
Hertfordshire WD25 8WT
Tel: 020 8950 0177
www.nawt.org.uk

Our Cats (magazine)
1 Lund Street
Manchester M16 9EJ
www.ourcats.co.uk

PDSA
Provides health advice and free veterinary services for pet owners on low incomes.
PDSA House
Whitechapel Way
Priorslee
Telford
Shropshire TF2 9PQ
Tel: 01952 290999
www.pdsa.org.uk

Pet Care Trust
Charity promoting responsible pet ownership.
Bedford Business Centre
170 Mile Road
Bedford MK42 9TW
Tel: 01234 273 933
www.petcare.org.uk

Pet Health Care
Online source of pet care information.
2nd floor Parkside
Horsham
West Sussex RH12 1XA
www.pethealthcare.co.uk

Pets as Therapy (PAT)
Charity providing therapeutic pet visits to hospitals and residential homes.
3a Grange Farm Cottages
Wycombe Road
Saunderton
Princes Risborough
Bucks HP27 9NS
Tel: 01844 345445
www.petsastherapy.org

Royal College of Veterinary Surgeons
UK regulatory body of the veterinary profession.
Belgravia House
62–64 Horseferry Road
London SW1P 2AF
Tel: 0207 222 2001
www.rcvs.org.uk

RSPCA
Investigates complaints of cruelty and rehomes animals through local branches.
Wilberforce Way
Southwater
Horsham
West Sussex RH13 9RS
Tel: 0300 12344 555
www.rspca.org.uk

Wood Green Animal Shelters
Animal welfare charity that provides shelter and rehoming services for unwanted and rescued animals.
601 Lordship Lane
Wood Green
London N22 5LG
Tel: 0844 248 8181
www.woodgreen.org.uk

Wood Green Animal Shelters (Cambridge)
King's Bush Farm
London Road
Godmanchester
Cambridgeshire PE29 2NH
Tel: 0844 248 8181
www.woodgreen.org.uk

Wood Green Animal Shelters (Heydon)
Highway Cottage
Heydon
Herts SG8 8PN
Tel: 0844 248 8181
www.woodgreen.org.uk

Index